MW00878333

Don't Believe
Everything You Think
Live in Joy!

John Beehner
Founder of Wise Counsel

By the Book Publishing
Jacksonville, Florida

This publication is designed to provide accurate and authoritative information in regard to the subject matter covered. It is sold with the understanding that neither the author nor the publisher is engaged in rendering legal, investment, accounting or other professional services. While the publisher and author have used their best efforts in preparing this book, they make no representations or warranties with respect to the accuracy or completeness of the contents of this book and specifically disclaim any implied warranties of merchantability or fitness for a particular purpose. No warranty may be created or extended by sales representatives or written sales materials. The advice and strategies contained herein may not be suitable for your situation. You should consult with a professional when appropriate. Neither the publisher nor the author shall be liable for any loss of profit or any other commercial damages, including but not limited to special, incidental, consequential, personal, or other damages.

First edition 2024

ISBN - 9798336992502

—Dedicated to —

I dedicate this book to my wonderful wife of 57 years, Judith Kiss Beehner. She loved me and was a fantastic wife, mother to our four children, an excellent teacher, excellent Pregnancy Crisis Counselor and a superstar Grandmother until her death in 2021. God put us together, and she endured my roller coaster ride of chasing success and seeking God's deepest will for us and our household. I am excited to see her in heaven when my journey is complete on earth.

I also want to thank my new wife, Nita, who has been an incredible support and encourager to help me complete this book and carve out a new life together til we are called home.

I also want to thank my kids who have believed in me and a greater purpose in me.

Blessings, John

Key Premise for the Book

Two Kinds of Wisdom

James 3:13-18 NIV

*13 Who is wise and understanding among you?
Let them show it by their good life, by deeds done in
the humility that comes from wisdom.
14 But if you harbor bitter envy and selfish ambition in
your hearts, do not boast about it or deny the truth. 15 Such
"wisdom" does not come down from heaven but is earthly,
unspiritual, demonic. 16 For where you have envy and selfish ambition, there you find disorder and every evil practice.*

*17 But the wisdom that comes from heaven is
first of all pure; then peace-loving, considerate,
submissive, full of mercy and good fruit, impartial
and sincere. 18 Peacemakers who sow in
peace reap a harvest of righteousness.*

What People Are Saying

"If you want to be a closer knowing your true calling, and want to help others grow, this book is for you! John has complied his personal, and many other testimonies, to inspire and to encourage all to, "Live life not just to get to heaven but to have heaven be part of your earthly experience." This book gives everyone an incentive and reason to push through obstacles.

As a School Administrator, Bible Teacher, and Christian Counselor, I found practical insight to change anyone's thinking process to praise with renewed hope. It's also a great guidebook to help other people grow by asking the right questions! A great read for those who want a sound doctrine with a life full or peace, love, and joy."

Susan Dyer, Bible teacher and Counselor

"In our mixed-up society today with a "Anything Goes" attitude perpetuated by evil desires, broken promises and selfish gains, it no wonder 80% of people are flooded with thoughts of fear or doubts that lead to health and spiritual issues. If you or a friend deal with these issues they need to read this tremendous book."

Sandra N. Love, Trainer, teacher Consultant and Professor

"I have worked with John and love this book. Too many people are trapped in their childhood fears or past failures. This book will inspire every reader on how to Find True Joy, peace, and love in their life. I am sharing copies."

Jodee Kulp,
Author, PraiseMoves Instructor, Biblical Health Coach

"John has been has been a Leader and Coach to many top CEOs and Ministry leaders and this book is a profound understanding on to get your heart, head, and spirit aligned with to the ultimate success in all you have designed to accomplished in a simplistic way."

Frank Ryll,
Past President of the Florida Chamber of Commerce.

"I wish I had read this book 30 years ago, it would have helped me overcome or deal with many crises and traumas in my life and career." We are not alone in our battles if we plan to help others overcome their fears, pride, stubbornness. I have helped John write other books but this one is truly inspiring and life changing"

Dr. Bill McCombes, CEO of Jesus Quest International

Table of Contents

-1-

Welcome to This Journey!

I would have never thought I would write a book about fear, confusion, and deceit.

One of my childhood memories is of the day that, as a third grader, I heard these words, ***"You should love your neighbors,"*** as our family was at church. I asked my mom, ***"How can we love our neighbors? We don't even know our neighbors."***

My mom said, ***"Oh, well, we love them."***

But I said, ***"We hardly ever speak to them."*** Then I said, ***"Is God ever going to talk to me?"***

And she said, ***"No, Johnny, you just have to be a good person, and that will get you to Heaven, and there you'll get to meet Him."***

There was a time when the milkman came from a local dairy and delivered milk to a family's doorstep, in our case, near the kitchen door. One morning, I asked if I could go outside and bring the milk in. I was excited as I picked up the half gallon of milk and opened the kitchen door. Unfortunately, the glass was wet with condensation. It slipped from my hands and fell onto the floor, smashing the glass. The milk covered the floor. I can still picture it as I write. Then I heard yelling from both my parents: ***"You bad boy! You bad boy!! Go to your room; there will be no milk for us!"***

Evil has loved reminding me
that I am BAD over and over again!

In my early years, my understanding of the Lord and evil was limited. Although I had a basic knowledge of Biblical principles and the Ten Commandments, church was more of a religious experience than a spiritual one.

I remember a college time (probably two years) when I felt led to pray as I got in bed, ***"God, please use me to make the greatest contribution to mankind I can make."*** It was a deep desire in my heart. I just hoped God heard my prayer. I now believe, many years later, that one prayer protected me from numerous kinds of potential harm.

My parents advised me that if I wanted to be successful, I should move to the next town, take the bigger paying opportunity, and not depend on my parents. I should just be dependent upon my abilities and talents. The first thing a good husband and father does is to be the best provider, encourager, and supporter while teaching basic values expressed with loving kindness and discipline.

So, that's what I tried to do.

I discovered I was a risk-taker and adventurer in high school and college. During my senior year in college, I hitchhiked through Europe one summer, where I met my beautiful wife on a ship to Rotterdam. She was on a tour, and I was hitchhiking through nine counties. That became a romance that led to our marriage. Then, we were off to our next adventure in the Peace Corps in Brazil for two years.

Back in the USA, I started my business career—five different jobs from town to town—but always ***chasing success***. I had chased success in business for almost 15 years, moving too often, probably, with my beautiful wife and four kids not giving up on me. My commitment to them was unwavering. I always strive to be the best provider, encourager, and supporter while teaching basic values expressed with loving kindness and discipline.

I felt no deep or spiritual encounter while attending a traditional church with my family. For 19 years, the church was a good community and friendship experience for our family. Believing Jesus died on the cross for my sins was easy to believe. I understood that at age ten, but wasn't sure it had to do with me. I was a good person to most people and thought that sin was murder, robbery, rape, etc.

I know now that sin is "missing the mark" God has for us. Yet,the Grace of Jesus by dying on the cross covers my mistakes with unmerited favor that I don't deserve until I seek His forgiveness.

In 1979, I left my position at the Chamber of Commerce and started a new Executive Leadership Programs to offer business management and motivational training programs.

During the first year of a slow start and frustration, I drove to an appointment with a major company one day and had a life-altering experience. As I drove, I saw a demon in the back of my mind, trying to attack me, but I wouldn't take it, so I tried to wrestle him down. It went back and forth until I arrived at my appointment. I got out of my car, totally gripped with fear. I didn't know what to do but to go to my appointment feeling very sick inside. I tried to brave my way through that meeting.

I couldn't care less about making a sale. I just wanted to get to my office and overcome the fear. When I told my wife, she thought I was crazy. She reminded me that I had spoken to countless audiences and assured me that I would overcome my fears and talk to people. So, I did what many people do: I turned on the television to get my mind onto something else.

After seeing the ***"bad news"*** reports on television, I stumbled onto a talk show with Demas Sharkarian, who was interviewing an attorney from Toronto, Canada. I'll never forget what the attorney said: ***"My whole life changed when I turned it over to Jesus Christ and stopped trying to live my life for myself and started living it for Him."***

My reaction: ***I thought Priests got paid to say things like that, but not Attorneys on national TV.***

It touched me, so I prayed and cried at that very moment. I had never heard that God is alive and active in people's lives. The next day, I attended a meeting of the Full Gospel Businessman's Fellowship where I heard the testimony of another man and his life-changing experience and how God was leading him to a new life of success.

I had an appointment in Ft. Lauderdale the following day, so I had to drive five hours. I took my King James Bible with me, which I rarely read. When I got to my Days Inn hotel room, I continued to pray, cry, and read my Bible. Then, I noticed a small New Testament paperback Bible on the dresser table. As I opened it, I said, ***"This Bible is much easier to read than the one I brought."***

As I read, I noticed that this Bible included ***"the Sinner's Prayer."*** I read that prayer with great sincerity and committed my life to serving Jesus Christ for the rest of my days. I didn't realize how life-changing that would be, but I prayed, cried, and surrendered everything to the Lord. I still have that book today.

My Ft. Lauderdale appointment was a no-show. That was fine because I just wanted to return home and find comfort in learning to seek the Lord. My heart felt different. I felt like a burden was lifted from me.

Then, just a week later, Full Gospel had another speaker come from Melbourne, Florida, and give his testimony, and they offered a prayer for those who wanted to give their life to Christ and those who wanted to receive the baptism of the Holy Spirit. I knew nothing about that, but my wife and I felt we should seek that prayer. To my wife (who had been praying to know Jesus), it meant I'd be at church every Sunday with her. We had yet to hear about the baptism in the Holy Spirit, with evidence of speaking in tongues.

Afterward, as we drove home, we felt the Lord telling both of us how He had healed our daughter of a blood disorder after we learned that she was anemic shortly after her birth at Johns Hopkins Hospital. They kept evaluating her by extracting blood out of her brain, which was a terrifying situation for us and our newborn daughter.

And then we remembered something that had happened years before. We remembered a neighbor we thought was a ***"holy roller lady."*** She had heard about our concern and came down one day and asked to pray for our child. The following week, my wife took our baby back to the hospital, and the doctor said the blood disorder was gone.

We thought nothing of it then, but the Lord reminded us of that moment in the car. It was the neighbor's prayer that made the difference. God had done a healing right there for us. That was another confirmation of the Holy Spirit working in us. We came together to recognize God was with us before we understood it.

My Breakthrough

As I shared, the first year of my new business was a struggle. My aim was not for fame or fortune but to create a home that met the needs of my wife, Judy, and our family. I aspired to serve people in the corporate training and education field, a path I had successfully experienced during my tenure at the Jacksonville, Florida, Chamber of Commerce. I anticipated that my business would offer similar rewards, but the journey was far from easy.

But within a few weeks of giving my life to Christ, I had booked a famous speaker from Dallas to speak at a conference to motivate and train four hundred managers at a large insurance company in Jacksonville.

However, a significant turning point came when the speaker's office called the day before his presentation to cancel his visit due to illness. They were sending someone in his place. As I hung up the phone, I felt a stirring within me, a voice whispering that this man was coming to deliver a message about my business. At that moment, I realized I had a spirit, and that God might have a plan to teach me something that would transform my business.

The speaker, **Don Wass**, did an excellent job. As we talked after his speech, I asked him about his business. As I listened, I realized I was already doing everything he was doing in his similar and successful business. However, I had yet to have significant success. But then He mentioned something called The Executive Committee (TEC), founded in Milwaukee in 1957, a small group where CEOs would come together to learn from each other, give advice, learn from experts about growth, and build friendships,

As he described it, I envisioned the Lord speaking to my heart and showing me six visions of that were already a part of my professional career. For example, I had led the Southern Spirit Council at my University, I had helped CEO's lead different committees to improve public schools, I sold memberships at Chambers of Commerce, ran the Leadership Greenville program, selected speakers and created business seminars to help with corporate training and small business "How to" workshops.

I saw immediately running The Executive Committee in Florida was my calling. Next how would it come together? Don agreed to call his friends at TEC to introduce me. I enthusiastically thanked Don and knew this was my calling, which I successfully did for the next 14 years.

I was blessed to get the license for Florida, which became a $2 million business serving nearly three hundred clients. The business is now called Vistage. The Lord called me to sell the company in 1995, write a book, and then eventually start Wise Counsel, a Christian program doing similar things, but one where we prayed together and had a heart for both business knowledge and more profound spiritual insights. That's how my journey started and why I am writing this book. My prayer is that it will be life-changing for you.

-2-

Early Education and Lies

I loved my parents. They were good people with good values, hard workers, loving, kind, and considerate. They allowed me to take risks and even learn from my mistakes. My dad demonstrated character by his hard work. He was the General Manager of a major company in Chicago for 20 years.

The same day that I asked my mom about loving our neighbors. I also asked her about evil, and she shared something that I finally realized was not true and very uninformed. She said there is no such thing as a devil, which was Halloween and cartoon stuff made up by different people. Anyone who reads the Bible realizes that's not true.

Another thing that happened in my early years was coming home to my mom and saying they called me names at school.

They called me ***"Beehner, the wiener,"*** and they called me ***"fatso,"*** and I felt so bad.

Mom tried to encourage me with her favorite statement:

"Sticks and stones may break your bones, but names or words will never hurt you."

Of course, through life, coming to Christ, and my passion to serve Him, I realized I have believed significant lies because they still live in me—subconsciously in my memory or soul. The enemy uses those "imprints on your mind" against you and me. The enemy reminds you and me of our fears, doubts, pains, and hurts with the plan often to deceive us – or worse – or be called BAD to control or limit us.

Anyone who has any encounter with Christ comes to realize we are in the midst of an evil world, as the Bible refers to, and there is a devil who's trying to take all of us down or keep us from achieving God's ultimate purpose in our lives. The enemy uses those old memories, those old value statements, to remind us how weak or inept we are, and we can never please God or ourselves.

I don't care who you are; you will hear things in your thought life that are not true, condemning, or troublesome. These things will produce fear and keep you from taking risks or loving others and how God intends. I love how the Bible talks about words in the book of Philippians.

—Philippians 4:8—

Finally, brothers and sisters, whatever is true,
whatever is noble, whatever is right, whatever is pure,
whatever is lovely, whatever is admirable—
if anything is excellent or praiseworthy
—think about such things.

Let me share how two other personal examples of evil can send us fearful messages of worry and doubts. These two unrelated traumatic events of death had such a profound impact on one person that changed the lives of thousands of people.

Can you see in the Darkness?

Pam Mullarkey, a naturally resilient educator, and leader, tells the story of a neighbor girl who approached her while jogging before going to work one morning.

The young girl asked Pam. *"Would you please tell the parents across the street that their daughter is pregnant and she's going to get an abortion."*

Pam explains how a flood of conflicting thoughts overwhelmed her mind. Her thoughts expressed disbelief about the situation; others expressed doubt and convinced her to act.

The experience reminded her of the tragedy that hit Pam and her family when her brother died. Etched into her psyche was a memory. She believed she had heard a condemning lie that told her she was the reason her brother had died. Like venom from a snake bite, that lying thought poisoned her body and soul with so much guilt and shame that it defined her for years. Those evil thoughts rang in her mind, battling over what to do about this young girl. Do I tell the neighbor about her daughter?

The debate was challenging for her. The competing voices all sounded rational and relentless.

"You are going to look stupid, like a nosy neighbor ... you have no right to interfere in their lives."

So, she decided to pray about it. After some time, it felt like God was saying to her, 'to tell them.'

Fear was gripping her as she rehearsed how to approach her neighbor. What would she say, and how would she react? Her thoughts said, *"You are going to look so stupid," and "she will never speak to you again. Your neighbor will attack you if you are wrong," After a couple of sleepless nights, she concluded, "The battle belongs to you, God. I cannot rest because you know the truth and you have a plan. This young girl needs your love and not to be labeled a* ***"slut"*** *and have more young boys take advantage of her."*

Pam chose courage over fear and decided to knock on the neighbor's door.

After welcoming comments, Pam said. *"Is there a chance that your daughter is pregnant?"*

The mother laughed out loud. *"Pam! She has never even had a date. She's only a freshman in high school, and we don't let her date!"*

Pam's response was, *"OK, well, her best girlfriend told me that she was going to have an abortion."*

Shocked but privately, the mother confronted her daughter and found out it was true…she was pregnant.

The young girl knew nothing about sex because her parents had not taught her. A football player wanted to take her on a date, but she was not allowed to date. He persisted and asked when he could see her.

"Well, maybe after school. You could come to my house after school but leave before 5:30 because my parents get home by 6 pm," she told him. He educated her quickly - all about sex. Then he told the other boys her phone number and how easy she was. She allowed others to come by the house while her parents worked.

Unfortunately, she did have an abortion, which disturbed Pam so much that she prayed. *"Lord, somebody should be doing something about this; kids don't know what they're doing; sex is not a game."*

As she prayed over the next three nights, the Lord answered. He would not let her go to sleep until she wrote out the plan He placed in her heart. Those events became the inspired plan to teach girls in high school about sex and avoid young men who were wrongly pursuing them.

The program became so successful that Northeast Florida schools included it in their high school curriculum. For 25 years, it impacted over 500,000 young girls in the USA, Russia, Uganda, the Dominican Republic, and more.

Eventually, Pam turned over Project SOS to the Boys and Girls Club.

So, what's the purpose of this example?

So, do you think straight?

There is a battle for our minds. The Lord has a plan for each of us to be successful through His will and purpose, and the enemy, the devil or Satan, wants to make sure we miss our calling.

We all can relate to having competing thoughts in our minds. But how do we know if they are directly from God, our logic, or directly from evil?

Was it easy for Eve in the garden to know the difference in the garden? Our problem is that we are not in control of our thinking. The purpose is to tell you it is time to be discerning about your thoughts of good or evil, fear or even condemnation, and the origin of your thoughts.

Have you heard this in church?

God is the Spirit of love, truth, and life. He is invisible to nearly all of us, but His Spirit lives in us. He created each of us by His Spirit and used our mother and father to conceive our physical body with its organs, bones, muscles, ligaments, etc. Plus, the soul is the mind, personality, will, and emotions (some refer to as flesh). When we die, the plan is for our spirit to go to Heaven, accomplishing His will in us.

Satan is a fallen angel of evil working to destroy God's plans and impact us all. Of course, we are born with the free will to decide who we will follow. The ***"world's ways"*** are full of evil, and selfishness compared to God's ways and His road to love, mercy, grace, and what is known as the "Fruit of the Spirit."

Christ came to save us from our sins and said we must be born of the Spirit (Born Again) to demonstrate our commitment to follow Him and the purpose for our lives. When we read the Bible and allow the Holy Spirit to come alive in our soul (mind, will, and emotions) we are showing our commitment.

For example, sometimes the name of someone who has greatly offended you or never pay a debt they owe to you. ***The Lord may convict (remind) your heart (Spirit and Soul) to forgive that person.*** You may first think (in your soul) *"No way."* But then the Holy Spirit will send you a message like this *"are you not blessed in your business of family? Jesus died on the cross for our sins just like He did for yours. And your unforgiveness could allow the power of evil to overcome one or both you."*

Going to him and saying I forgive you may change his whole life and be a great breakthrough.

This is seeing though the power of the Holy Spirit.

Gaining spiritual eyes and begin to see as God sees as we pray and seek His face and ways. That's when we gain peace of mind. When we choose God's ways, we find that these ways are very different from Satan's.

— John 3:16 —

For God so loved the world that he gave
his one and only Son, that whoever believes in him, shall
not perish but have eternal life.

—1 Corinthians 2:14-15 —

The person without the Spirit does not accept the
things that come from the Spirit of God but considers the
foolishness and cannot understand them because they
are discerned only through the Spirit. The person with
the Spirit makes judgments
about all things, but such a person is not
subject to merely human judgments,

Academy Award winner **Denzel Washington** has said, *"We are in a Spiritual Battle. So, I look at things from an Eternal Perspective. If you don't have a Spiritual Foundation, you will easily be swayed by whatever way the wind blows."*

So, Satan can and does impact our thinking and create fear, evil, and doubts.

Our life experiences, family, youth, faith, business, job or entertainment, and culture influence us. Those influences are what mental health counselors call core beliefs. These are inherent biases we don't even recognize we have. A seven-year-old child's actions and attitudes reflect the personality traits that the child was born with.

You may experience them as ***"Stinking Thinking,"***… as **Zig Ziglar** used to say. Doubts and negative thoughts flood our minds.

For example: When you're going to make a decision or even have a random conversation with someone, different thoughts run through your mind; these thoughts are programming from your core beliefs. These core beliefs become automatic thoughts.

— 1 Corinthians 13:11 —

When I was a child, I spoke like a child,
I thought like a child, I reasoned like a child.
When I became a man, I gave up childish ways.

So, the Battle is for my Soul and Spirit?

I have discovered that we hear three voices in our heads, which impact our:

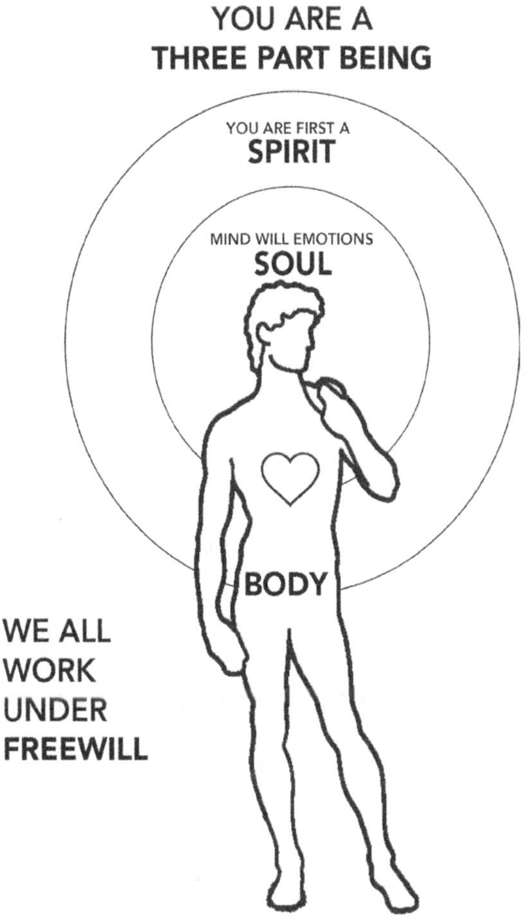
YOU ARE A
THREE PART BEING
YOU ARE FIRST A
SPIRIT
MIND WILL EMOTIONS
SOUL
BODY
WE ALL
WORK
UNDER
FREEWILL

- ✓ **Soul**, which is our mind, will, personality, and emotions
- ✓ **Spirit**, which is how we connect with the Lord, our Creator, who has a plan for each of our lives. This is embodied in the Holy Spirit of God.
- ✓ **Flesh and Pride**: Our beliefs, experiences in everyday life, and parental values we learned or failed to learn influence us. It is the good and bad of this world, our family heritage, our accomplishments, and our failures that are the determining factors of who we are. Through this we have achieved or lost self-confidence.

Evil's goal is to condemn you with fear, doubts, criticism and keep off track from God's purpose in you.

Why many people don't believe there is a God?

We live in a Physical Body with a Soul and Mind.
Outside of Church very few people recognize
we have a Spirit, which is the main part of our life.
Yet Evil does its best to keep us ignorant to the
fact we have a Spirit. God is a Spirit.
You won't see Him with your earthly EYES.
Many people will say...
I can't see God! So if He is not visible ...
So He is not real. Thus there is no reason to pray for or ask for help or guidance. I will live for myself and do whatever I like or can get away with.
The truth is God sent Himself through his Son Jesus to make a physical appearance on earth. To show and relate to us physically and demonstrate some of His powers, love and compassion for each of us. He died on the cross to forgive us of our ignorance, past and future sins of the world to allow all people to live a better life. ***"This is the main reason why mankind has made major strides over the last the last 2024 years in the midst of evil."*** He will break further the power of evil for those who turn to Him for His love in a new life knowing His calling for each of us.
His Holy Spirit embodies His words.

The Lord's goal is to love, encourage and fill you with love, peace, and joy. This is the Fruit of the Spirit—your gift to help you accomplish His purpose for you.

Can you recognize these paradoxical thoughts used by evil that become fears, doubts, and comments from critics? Is there an evil message in our thought life, inherited thoughts, or thinking from the sins of our parents/ancestors?

You have heard those basic condemning evil thoughts — "The Fiery Darts of the enemy" — you have listened to…in your mind. Have you had these thoughts? Reactions?

Check the box that you have heard in your mind.

___ You're a loser…stop trying to bluff your way…

___ You're not smart enough… you'll never make it.

___ They don't care about you…take some more drugs.

___ Don't embarrass yourself…no one cares anyway.

___ You are going to look stupid…get wasted with more beer.

___ No one loves you…just commit suicide.

___ You are sick and tired, don't try, just quit.

___ You always screw up...get drunk, take drugs to numb you.

___ You are a fool to keep trying.

___ They don't want your opinions.

___ You are stupid; don't think God will help you.

___ Better stop praying, or you will be late.

Yet, The opposite is true. ***If your Spirit is alive in Christ, the Lord's convicting, and loving thoughts, will guide you*** so that you will hear as you seek Him deeper and deeper through His words.

These are the things God wants to say to you.

- ✓ I love you and want to love you more.
- ✓ My job is knowing, loving, and guiding you like a mother and father.
- ✓ I created you for such a time as this.
- ✓ I have great plans for you: pursue my calling.
- ✓ I will give you visions and dreams.
- ✓ Bless those you meet with goodness and kindness.
- ✓ Honor your father and mother and your heritage.
- ✓ Forgive those who sin against you.
- ✓ Consider it all joy when you face trials and temptations.

- ✓ Seek me in times of fear or temptation.
- ✓ I will give you rest and peace of mind.
- ✓ I allow evil for you to search for my purpose in you.
- ✓ Your prayers will bear much fruit.
- ✓ Praise my name during a crisis; to calm you.
- ✓ I have angels guarding over you.
- ✓ Expect my healing power during pain.

Which Gate? Resentment or Forgiveness?

Most people recognize **Jim Carrey** as an actor, comedian, and witty personality on TV and in movies, expecting to laugh when he performs. He is very entertaining. So, it's very interesting to find his latest public video and profound statement coming from a man who has faced many challenges.

Without question, the difficulties of his life have allowed him to gain wisdom.

"I've had some challenges myself in the last couple of years, and they've led to some suffering. Well, ultimately, I believe suffering leads to something evil. We somehow must accept and not deny but feel our suffering."

"Then," he continues, *"we must make one of two decisions."*

"We either decide to either go through the gate of resentment, these dimensions, which leads to vengeance

and self-harm, which leads to harming others, or we can go to the gate of forgiveness, which leads to Grace as Christ did on the cross suffering terribly, and he was broken by it yet looked upon those people who were causing that suffering with compassion, with forgiveness and that's what opens the gates of heaven."

Does this apply to you?

Listening to a small voice during failure

James Kraft peddled cheese on his horse-drawn wagons. During his early days in Chicago, he became discouraged because sales were poor, and capital was exhausted. He heard a voice saying, ***'You are a failure.'*** One day, he let his mind be free of the frantic planning that had exhausted him. It was a receptive interlude and distinct conviction:

"You have been working without God." He said, "I stopped and listened for the first time. I had been able to stop hearing the words that must have been spoken to my ears repeatedly. So, I resolved to let God have direction in my life, and from that moment forward, my life began to change, and in every way, defeat was impossible. God had

provided me with invincible assets. I have never stopped listening since."

After James Kraft's business became a phenomenal success, he became a great spokesman for God working in one's life. He said, "In the stillness of spirit, a man is listening, heart and mind. I became conditioned spiritually for divine guidance, and the second most direct *route to inspiration is the daily systematic habit of reading the word of God. It speaks directly to men and women, powerfully and personally, when they read the Bible daily. I am convinced."*

Does this give you any ideas?

Corporate Healing and Turnaround

In the 1990s, **Tom Hill** took over the leadership of his father-in-law's company, Kimray, which manufactured parts for oil rigs. They were facing tough new competition from the Japanese. With $25 million in sales and 250 employees, his bottom line was hemorrhaging he was losing money fast. Workers' Compensation expenditures and employee turnover cost him millions of dollars a year.

He seriously considered closing the business. He

prayed and prayed and finally told his brothers in his Bible study. Some suggested that even if you lose people, they can become better father and mothers if you at least teach them about the character and nature of God.

He used ***49 Character Traits of God*** found in the Bible by the Basic Life Principles Institute as a guide. He then asked managers from each department to recognize outstanding employees for exemplifying those character principles on the job. During company-wide meetings, management recognized those employees with a certificate honoring their contribution to the company.

This practice not only changed the company's culture but also *reduced employee turnover and worker compensation by 80% despite raises and the increased cost of materials.* Profits went to their highest levels. Employee spouses saw a difference between their husbands and wives and thanked the company.

God's principles work. My business, Wise Counsel, and ministry has numerous stories and examples like these to share with leaders who want to walk deeper in His Ways.

Does this apply to you?

What is the greatest tool God has given mankind?

1997, while writing my first book, the Lord asked me that question. I humbly and prayerfully asked Him, and He answered me. The answer flooded and inspired this book.

The greatest tool God has given mankind are Words.

— Hebrew 4:12 —

"The Word of God is sharper than two edge swords, and it cuts through darkness and evil."

— Matthew 4:4 —

"It is written: 'Man shall not live on bread alone,
but on every word that comes from
the mouth of God.'"

— Luke 11:28 —

"Blessed rather are those who hear the
word of God and obey it."

God and Jesus are embodied in His Words

The Spirit of God is in His words and our shield. The Bible is His words, commands, and directions. Words are in sounds, they can condemn, praise, heal, torment, and inspire.

Words are …Jesus said in Matthew 6:63 (NIV), *"The Spirit gives life; the flesh counts for nothing. The words I have spoken to you are full of the Spirit and life."*

If you just believe Christ died on the cross for the world and it doesn't really relate to your life or if you think something like, ***"I am not really a big sinner"***, you are missing the depth of what Christ has said. We have all sinned in our mind or actions. You are spirit first created by the one True Spirit. God and Jesus Christ. You can go to church every day of your life and not come alive in YOUR SPIRIT until you ask for forgiveness and ask the Lord to lead you. That is when you will Spirit will overcome the Flesh and Soul.

Words are thoughts, definitions, and sound containers of feelings, emotions, knowledge, wisdom, commands, directions, inspiration, and life for the Body, Soul, and Spirit. They can also be hatred, jealousy, bitterness, fear, resentment, and the worst of our thinking.

Genesis 1:28 tells us, ***"Be Fruitful and Multiply"*** to take on His nature and character. God's desire for us is that we follow His ways; and take on His character and actions. He wants us to take risks, be fruitful in our plans, ideas, crops, work, and families. He wants us to fulfill the visions and desires He sends to you. He created Heaven and earth and everything in it. He wants to love you and be loved in return.

Words move us and use and embody His nature.

— Proverbs 18:21 —

"The tongue has the power of life and death, and those who love it will eat its fruit."

— Proverbs 15:2 —

"The tongue of the wise adorns knowledge, but the mouth of the fool gushes folly."

— Proverbs 15:4 —

"The soothing tongue is a tree of life, but a perverse tongue crushes the spirit."

Taming the Tongue

— Philippians 4:8 —

"Finally, brothers and sisters, whatever is true, whatever is noble, whatever is right, whatever is pure, whatever is lovely, whatever is admirable—if anything is excellent or praiseworthy—think about such things."

— 1 Corinthians 2:14,15 —

"The person without the Spirit does not accept the things that come from the Spirit of God but considers them foolishness and cannot understand them because they are discerned only through the Spirit."

The person with the Spirit makes judgments about all things, but such a person is not subject to merely human judgments.

The Bible tells us that ***God and Jesus are the Word*** (John 1:1). Scripture invites and compels us to relate to our thought life, our decisions, our emotions, and our feelings to the written Word.

Years ago, I met **Jan Christie**, an incredible woman of faith and intercessor. She would call me sometimes and say, *"The Lord told me to call and pray for you today,"* and I would say, *"WOW...Thank you!"* I would ask, *"So God talks to you every day when you ask, and she said yes,"* That built my faith. I started asking God daily what scripture to read and what to think. I began to say it every morning...then I got bolder and said (as I still do today). *"Everything I think, say, and do has to come from you, Lord, I want to be obedient to your purpose. I don't want to stop and pray but to be an open vessel."*

I want to be open to His leading - all the time.

The Scriptures and the Word touch my heart and give me spiritual wisdom and discernment as God draws me closer to Him.

As a young man in college, I had no more than a 3rd-grade level of grounding in Christianity. Sunday school was a part of my life as a child. When I was a teenager, that went away even though I had been baptized as a ten-year-old. I developed a hunger for God in my early 20's. Every night for at least two years, I would pray: ***"Lord, use me to make the greatest contribution to mankind***

that I can." At the time, I had no idea what that might be or whether God was listening.

So, with all these things I share, I have had no seminary experience, no individual teaching about the Word of God. As you read further, I think you will agree I got a master's degree in "rough spots of life". I have chased success many times in many towns and had a lot of failures. My failures have drawn me closer to knowing God's plan every time.

The book of James talks about being a teacher. The word Rabbi means teacher; teaching means bringing out a disciple in Latin. Because we all have a role of teaching one another and sharing, we have a body, soul, and spirit with a business owner or even an employee or trainee. So, what is the spirit of God saying to us? It is how to change and become more effective so that we can serve Him more deeply and have peace amid a battleground of evil messages.

I have found an untold secret that I want to share. So be diligent with the end of this book. How do we discern?

Could you make a new shoe?

Bill Bowerman was an outstanding track coach. In addition to coaching at the University of Oregon, during the 1950's, he coached an Olympic Team. Yet he was constantly frustrated with the injuries to his athletes. He attributed their issues to the hard, yet flimsy shoes sold to track athletes. The injuries could often be related to their shoes. They had ankle problems, shin splints, hamstrings, etc. He sat at his kitchen table, considering different ideas and concepts until God led him to design a new shoe that would be lighter, more comfortable, and more flexible. He tried to sell the idea to local companies without success. And through frustration, doubt, and anger, he gave up the idea.

One day, with half his runners hurting, he prayed and shared scripture with his athletes to encourage them.

— 1 Corinthians 9:24 —

"Do you not know that all the runners run in a race, but only one gets the prize? Run in such a way as to get the prize."

In other words, run to win and do your best. Bowerman told his players that running is the same advice applied to all aspects of their lives.

As he drove home, he felt the Lord telling him that scripture was for him, too. He needed to go back and not quit on the vision for a new shoe of soft material. He used his waffle iron to make the indentations in a mock-up. It was as if God was saying ***to keep persevering, and somehow, he would get those shoes made, even if he had to do it himself.***

So, he handcrafted several pairs of shoes on the kitchen table for some of his runners to try out, and their response was very encouraging. His miler, **Phil Knight**, became very enthused about the shoes.. After graduating from Stanford with an MBA, Phil found shoemakers who could manufacture the shoes and sold them out of his pickup truck to different coaches. Little did Bill and Phil know they were creating a new industry. They picked the name Nike, ***"the Greek God of swiftness."***

Our God is the God who gives visions. Their creation has changed the shoe industry, and Nike is a 50-billion-dollar company today.

Is God speaking to you too?

Is there something in your life you need to persevere through?

What is one step you can take to move forward?

Be in the World, but not of the World, but of a changed Spirit, Love of God, Grace, Suffering with Christ

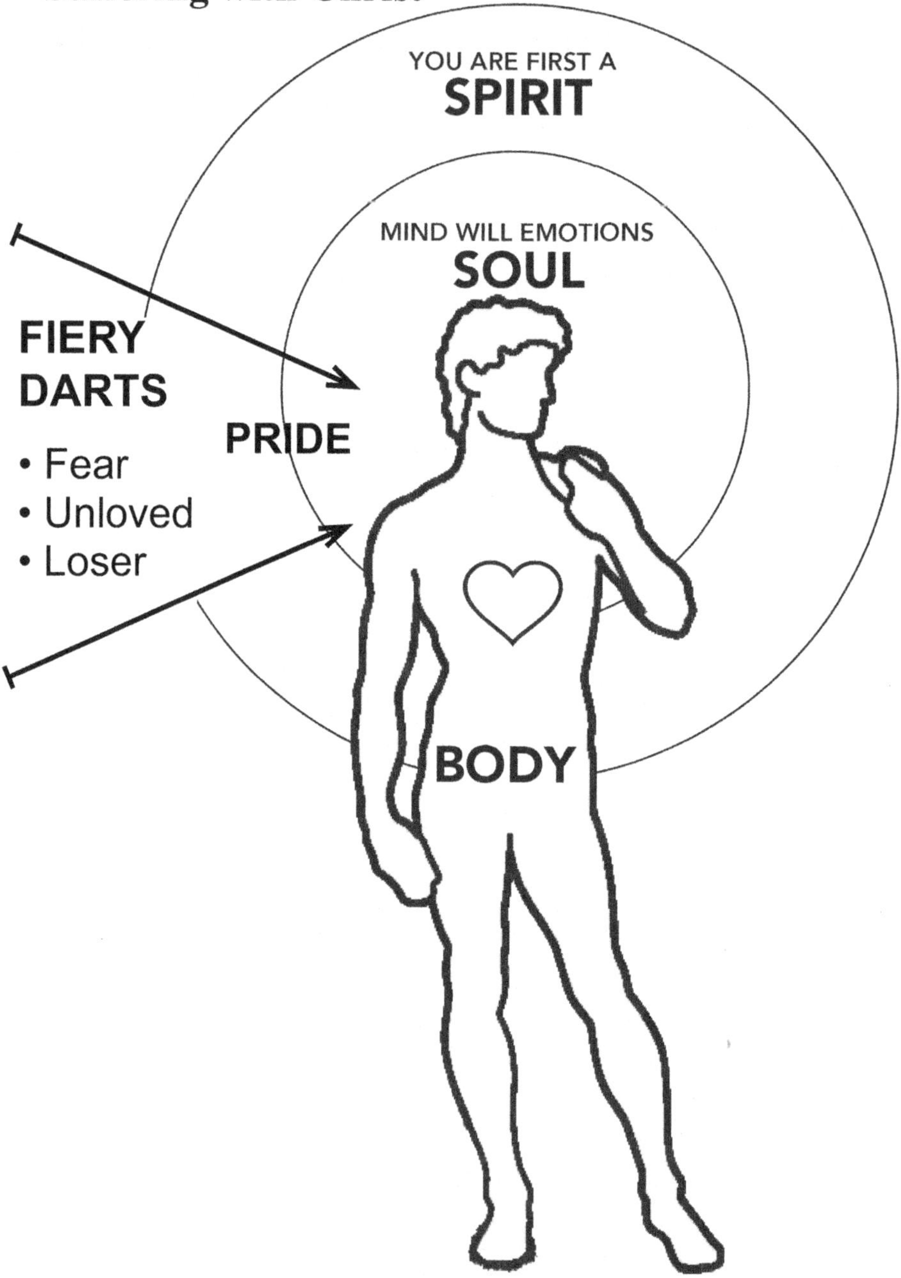

God is His Words
If you abide in Him — He will live in you

What are Golden Rule stores?

James Cash Penney's father was a Pastor who told his son ***"Always treat people with the golden rule."*** The elder Penney was a farmer who had been fired from his church. That did not prevent him from having a right attitude as he encouraged his son. Young Jim moved on to Kemmerer, Wyoming, which was a mining town. He worked in a small retail shop that he later bought. He gave the store managers a share of the profits. Retailers were notorious for charging whatever they wanted, raising prices based on how much they thought the shopper had. Jim refused to do that. Instead, he marketed fair prices and even took returns, which became standards in the retail industry over time. Those stores became known as the **"Golden Rule"** stores, and he shared profits with employees. The rapidly growing business, by this time 175 stores, went public, and Penney moved the headquarters to Texas. Today, the business is known as the JCPenney Company.

Eventually, because of his rapid success, wealth, and notoriety, Penney stepped aside as CEO and partnered with different businesses. When the great depression of the late 1920s hit, he lost nearly everything. A doctor friend in Battle Creek, Michigan, noticed he had shingles and asked him to go to a sanitarium. That first night, Jim's pain was unbearable. Surely, he was dying. He wrote a letter to his wife, asking for forgiveness for all the lost money. He awoke hearing singing. It was a Salvation Army church service. He was broken, and tears of remorse were on his cheeks. He felt humiliated, a failure, a loser; he had failed his wife and family. He went to the service. He felt the power of God come all over him. He recognized that God was protecting him through tough times and that God was growing his business. He accepted the fact that his destiny was to go back to the business and be a witness for Christ for the rest of his days. He passed away at 96. He had lived another forty years!

Will God extend your life
for a greater purpose?

-3-

We Learn From Faith, Risk and Adversity

"And we know that for those who love God, all things work together for good, for those who are called according to his purpose," (Romans 8:28).

Mark **Burnett,** the legendary TV Producer who immigrated from England and is a dedicated Christian who is the producer of Survivor, The Apprentice, Shark Tank, The Voice, and The Cable TV series, The Bible, said that ***"Most men fear Regret—long-term things they did not accomplish in their lives. Others Fear looking stupid through failure."***

Burnett continued, ***"Coming to the USA was a big risk, but I realized that failing in America is OK. I was willing to look stupid to risk and fail rather than not trying at all. Everyone who succeeds will fail at some things."***

Rollo May, author of ***Man's Search for Himself,***

said, ***"The opposite of courage is not cowardice, its conformity."***

Thomas Edison said, ***"I found 6,000 ways not to make a light bulb, but some risks will succeed if you keep trying and learn from past mistakes."***

Tom Watson, the former CEO who once built IBM into a large and successful company with 400,000 employees, said, ***"Successful companies make mistakes faster to find the right products and services that customers want and need."***

In my 1980 experience of being attacked by a demon and finding Christ, I was facing incredible fear and torture inside of me. I learned so much from one scripture that gave me eternal peace of mind; the more I read it, the more I understood it. It sank into my soul and spirit.I repeat this scripture here:

— 1 Corinthians 2:14-16 —

"The person without the Spirit does not accept the things that come from the Spirit of God but considers them foolishness and cannot understand them because they are discerned only through the Spirit. The person with the Spirit makes judgments about all things, but such a person is not subject to merely human judgments, for, "Who has known the mind of the Lord to instruct him? But we have the mind of Christ."

I had been foolish - only operating in my selfish state of mind, chasing the world's way of defining success for me over what was my calling and that God had created me for. First as a spirit, then with a soul (my mind, will, personality, and emotions). I was a three-part being body, soul, and spirit. The Lord was waiting for me to understand and walk deeper into my real purpose in life. I could not see a spirit, but God was starting to show me as He became alive in me and influenced me.

One of my highlights was working with two company CEOs who grew from $2 million in sales to $2 billion and were winners of the Horatio Alger Award. There, I met Quincy Jones, Dave Thomas of Wendy's, Ted Turner, and Truett Cathy of Chick-fil-A, founder. Later, I had Pat Robertson speak to us, telling us how he founded the Christian Broadcasting Network (CBN).

Being called to work with over 300 CEOs and Executives in that way was divine intervention. It was God's leading and calling to prepare me to help people grow their businesses, manage more daily tactical and long-term strategic issues, and receive more fulfillment and satisfaction from growth and problem-solving.

Years later, I met the 92-year-old founder of **The Executive Committee (TEC), Bob Nourse,** in Milwaukee and learned that he came to Christ when both his father and brother died, and the family lost their manufacturing company.

He prayed daily, ***"O Lord, what can I do with my life."*** For over a year, he sought counsel from his priest. He believed that the Lord gave him a vision and fundamental principles that he felt he should share with others. From that experience, he founded and operated The Executive Committee.

The principles have mostly stayed the same today. As happens so often, tragedy opens new doors and causes us to seek God's will. He loved to learn and was a good facilitator of small groups. The Executive Committee (TEC) now operates in 35+ countries, and at least 45,000 CEOs and executives are involved. Today, the business is known as Vistage.

Like Pam Mullarkey, we have examples that show how the Holy Spirit is trying to lead us. Adversity is our teacher; when we learn the wisdom of our pain, the pain can go away. At the same time, our bodies, minds, and hearts bear the scars of tragedy resulting from healing. It is priceless.

-4-

What are Treasures Buried in Your Heart?

In my world of guiding entrepreneurs and ministry leaders, I've witnessed countless founders and CEOs who, guided by the Holy Spirit, embark on the journey of starting or expanding a business or ministry. Their courage and determination are truly inspiring.

"Every business is ministry, and every ministry Is a business." This concept emphasizes the need to 'LOVE' with kindness to our customers, employees, suppliers – actually, all with whom we come in contact. It is about treating them with respect while generating revenue to grow by building a good reputation. In essence, it's about conducting business in a way that reflects the values and teachings of our faith.

Organizations that lie or
deceive people can't survive.

Truett Cathy, the founder of Chick-fil-A, started the Dwarf House near Atlanta after World War II. It was at the Dwarf House that the idea of serving a chicken breast on a roll was developed. Cathy was so committed to the Lord that he refused to open on Sundays for two reasons. First, it is the Lord's Day, one of rest and observing the Sabbath as stated in the Ten Commandments. Second, he was committed to leading a Bible study for young men in his church. Thousands attested to his teaching, which helped them become men of integrity.

But in the early 2000s, the tremendous growth of Chick-fil-A in free-standing stores became a competitor, like McDonald's, Wendy's, and a myriad of fast-food restaurants, as they recognized they were losing business and needed to sell chicken to compete. For the first time in their history, Chick-fil-A had stopped growing. Truett saw that as a crisis, so he asked his best advisors for three days of prayer and strategizing.

The result was a Corporate Mission Statement:
"To glorify God by being a faithful steward of all entrusted to us. To have a positive influence on all who come in contact with Chick-fil-A."

That statement would be posted in every restaurant to show their dedication to serving the Lord. Today, the headquarters staff prays for all the restaurants, and they are growing at nearly a billion dollars a year, outpacing all their competitors, who are open seven days a week.

There are an equal number of examples from ministry leaders. **Francis McNutt** was a Catholic priest called by God to describe how people can ask and receive healing from prayer. It led him to leave the priesthood and marry his wife, Judith. Together, they formed the **Christian Healing Ministry (CHM)**, which, for more than 30 years, has taught and demonstrated God's heart in healing to thousands worldwide. Their key to success is hearing from the Holy Spirit. Examples of other profound groups are Campus Crusade for Christ, founded by **Bill Bright**; Youth with a Mission (YWAM), **Loren Cunningham**; Go to Nations, **Daniel Williams**, founder; and Habitat for Humanity which was founded by **Millar Fuller** and his wife.

Cash is not King.

In the 1920s, **Conrad Hilton** struggled with his first significant hotel in Dallas, yet people saw his gift and talent for raising money. He could impress bankers and make deals happen and had built a chain of 12 hotels before the Great Depression. The business was starved of cash, yet he refused to declare bankruptcy. Hilton knew his good name and credit rating were vital to his business.

Collections, fear, doubts, threats, and lawsuits plagued him. A supplier to whom he had once owed $100,000 and faithfully paid each month, sued him for only $178. His hotel ownership eroded, yet miraculously, he avoided bankruptcy several times despite collections, fear, doubts, lawsuits, and threats. One of his employees believed so much in him that he gave Conrad his $300 savings to help the company.

Hilton stuck to the long-ago advice of his mother: ***"Some men jump out of windows, and some quit and go to church. Conrad, you should pray and pray harder and don't dare give up."*** Conrad went to church every day before work for prayer. Hilton believed that prayer was the answer.

He said, ***"It's our means of communication with God. You can speak to Him anytime, night or day, and know with certainty that he is listening to you; there are no call letters. You're free to send a message. You, God, want me to first live by filling out my place in the world and faithfully using my talents. Each of these is in the cycle of successful living. Prayer is the hub that holds the whole wheel together. Without constant prayer with God, we are nothing."***

Do we chisel our way to success?

These leaders sacrificed their worldly calling of success to find the Lord's real heart for their service.

The word character in Greek means to chisel. So, is God allowing adversity or Satan and evil thoughts to chisel away at your false thinking or facade? [Michelangelo carved David; he just chipped away what wasn't David"]

— Romans 5:3-5 —

"Not only so, but we also glory in our sufferings because we know that suffering produces perseverance; perseverance, character; and character, hope. 5 And hope does not put us to shame, because God's love has been poured out into our hearts through the Holy Spirit, who has been given to us."

Trials and Temptations

— James 1:2-8 —

"Consider it pure joy, my brothers and sisters, whenever you face trials of many kinds, 3 because you know that the testing of your faith produces perseverance. Let perseverance finish its work so that you may be mature and complete, not lacking anything. If any of you lacks wisdom, you should ask God, who gives generously to all without finding fault, and it will be given to you. But when you ask, you must believe and not doubt, because the one who doubts is like a wave of the sea, blown and tossed by the wind. That person should not expect to receive anything from the Lord. Such a person is double-minded and unstable in all they do."

— Luke 11:28 —

"Blessed rather are those who hear the word of God and obey it."

Born in Cleveland, Ohio, in the 1860s, **Henry Crowell** was the son of a shoe merchant who died from tuberculosis at the young age of 43. This was devastating to Henry, for he not only would not be able to go to Yale University as he had planned, but he also had inherited the potential to contract TB. The doctor sent him west to clear his lungs from the Ohio steel mills.

Henry had recently committed his life to serving Christ, and his friends were praying with him to seek God's will. In fear and trembling, he realized the Biblical significance of a doctor giving a seven-year order. He believed there had to be a divine purpose for his struggle and battle to breathe normally. Those years were frightening, and he had no money or security, but he worked odd jobs on ranches and farms. He gained experience in business by buying, planting, and selling two farms in North Dakota.

He pledged that if the Lord would allow him to make money in a business, he would keep his name off the company so that God would get the glory. As he finally returned home, he continually overcame doubt and fear. Within 30 days of being home, Crowell learned of a run-down mill near Akron. He prayed, listened for the Lord's voice, and made the purchase, which became a giant and a legend in the food industry, **Quaker Oats**. His experience as a farmer paid off!

-5-

How God Can Change a Heart.

M**ax Karrer**, noted Obstetrician and Gynecologist who was on the first Memorial Hospital Board, was instrumental in the founding of Community Hospice and a local church. The only issue was that he and other doctors on his staff performed abortions. All the doctors liked it because they made a substantial amount of money. He saw no problem until he went on a church retreat. There, he was confronted by what the Bible said about life.

The Holy Spirit began to convict him in such a way that he resigned from his group practice. Then, he started to share his decision with the community and stood firm against abortion. He spoke at local clubs, and I used his testimony on Inspiration 316 in 2018.

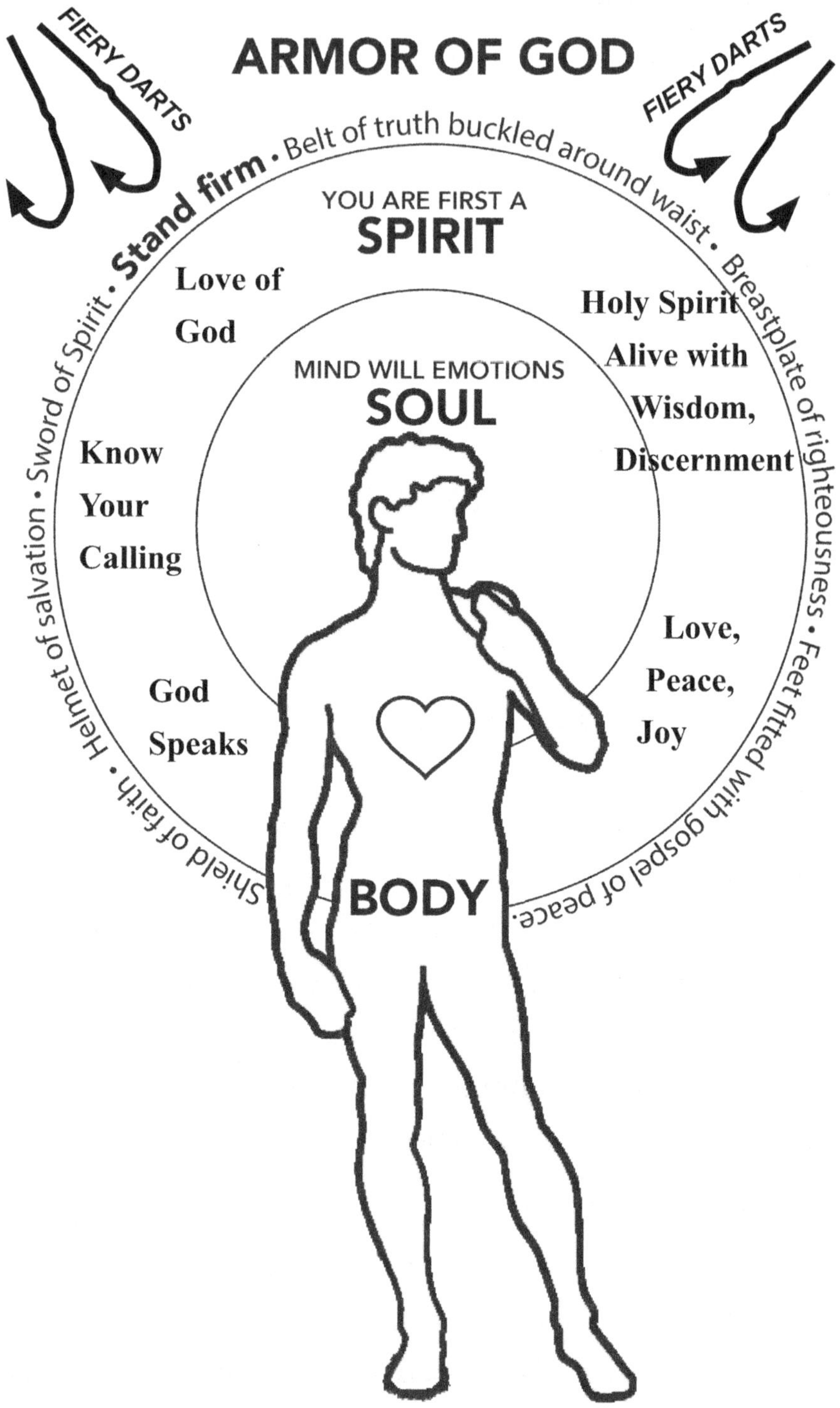

Take on the Armor of God
Learn Him Through His Book

His convictions led him to be the Florida state chairman of the Christian Coalition and to join the Board of the Christian Broadcasting Network with Pat Robertson and the Right to Life group.

Is God calling you to be a leader, a risk taker, a CEO, a business leader, or a ministry leader? Understanding God's call for our lives can often feel elusive and intangible. We may have placed obstacles in our path, making it hard to hear God's voice. But instead of questioning Him, we must be obedient to everything God tells us to do, even if we don't fully understand it. We must persevere and have faith in His plan; as scripture says, teachers are held to a higher standard.

One of the most profound things I've learned through business and God's revelation has been studying the Parable of the Sower, which is repeated in Matthew, Mark, and Luke in the New Testament. I consider it a road map to success for anyone called to be an obedient leader.

Have you not had a great idea and said, ***"Oh, I'd love to do that, but I can't…I don't have the money, I don't have the time, I'm not smart enough, I don't have the contacts to make that work."***

Yes, God is asking people to take risks. He is the creator, giving visions through His character and nature (Genesis 1:28) of his word and leading his Holy Spirit. He's testing us. He places it in the pathway of your soul.

How do you respond?

Sometimes, you say. ***"I had that idea before, but I could never do anything about it."***

— Proverbs 25:2 —

"It is the Glory of God to conceal the matter;
to search out a matter is the glory of kings."

This means God is seeking people who hunger for His leading, things hard to find because they prove to be the real kings in His eyes — those He wants to reward.

Does this apply to you?

So, the Parable of the Sower represents the calling of God through His Seed.

The seed is a word of God in a vision and purpose leading through those with Spiritual lenses, which refers to the ability to perceive and understand God's will and guidance. God impregnates us with an idea, calling, vision, or mission. Sometimes, we don't accept it, and we miss out on His leading. Of course, it is a battle with what the enemy or our ignorance is trying to keep us caught up in our pride, inabilities, and perceived weaknesses.

To summarize Matthew 13:3-23 ***A farmer went out to sow his seed, and as he was scattering the seeds, some fell on the path, and the birds came and took it away. Then, some seeds fell on rocky places where the soil was shallow. But the plant was scorched and withered when the sun rose because it had no good roots. Other seeds fell on thorns, which grew up but were choked by weeds and thorns. Finally, the seed fell on good soil, producing the crop 30 or 60 times what had been shown before.*** This parable teaches us the different responses to God's calling and the risks involved.

Here is my interpretation of the Parable of Sower—the ***seeds are the visions, the ideas, unions, and the leading of the Lord***. He places them in our souls, which can touch our hearts/spirits so that we can take risks with new ideas. Sometimes, early financial investment is called 'Seed Capital,' which refers to the initial funding required to start a project or business. There are 83 references to the word Seed in the Bible.

So, when the ***first seed "idea" falls on the beaten-down soil,*** and we receive it, we may say, ***"A great idea. Somebody should do something about that, but not me. I don't have the capital, knowledge, time, or patience."***

In 1972, I saw a vision. I now look back and think it was an excellent preparatory experience. Everyone was talking about recycling, but very few were doing anything about it. I envisioned our neighborhood garbage truck coming to pick up our garbage in a large Rubbermaid® can with three compartments. One was for regular waste of food; another part was for paper (we had a newspaper at the time), and the other was for cans and plastics. The garbage man would empty into the truck while those items would flow into the truck and STAY separated. I spent $1800 with a patent attorney, had drawings made, and then traveled to Houston and El Paso, Texas, to visit recycling plants. I tried to talk to Rubbermaid, but they didn't pay any attention. Companies will often avoid inventors who they must pay royalties for the license and patent. So, I finally quit and did other innovative things for my employer.

Sometimes, the Lord can call on us to test our openness to things that prove unsuccessful but are part of our preparatory and faith-filled experience to get to the next level of opportunity or soil.

People without the spirit of God active in their lives will often quit too soon.

The ***second seed falls on the shallow soil.*** It grows but withers away, just like people who start a business or work to be authors or innovators and quit.

"OK, it's not working. I can't sustain this. I'm not smart enough; I just want you to think."

So, you give up.

The ***third level is where the seed falls among the thorns.*** What are the thorns? Think of them as a competitive group of businesses or a challenging task requiring effort and energy. However, as the Bible indicates, ***"Once your crop or grass is strong enough and healthy then you can start weeding out the weeds."***

Finally, ***you reach good soil worthy of the vision.*** You recognize that this is God's spirit working within you. Now, your maturity levels will allow you a position of influence as a teacher, songwriter, company leader, or school principal. You feel comfortable. You can accept the joy of knowing this is your calling. God has been working through you, but you have struggled. There are more positive thoughts replacing the garbage that has cluttered your mind. You are recognizing your greatest reward.

The opportunities for service are endless: ***"So the seed fell in the rocky soil."*** Our mind represents all the soils; the rocky soil is better than a beaten path but not good fertile soil. But if you have matured, you are more open to risk, seeking something to get ahead. The Neuropathways in your brain have some rocky places. But you say. ***"That's a good idea; I can try that."*** It is not abnormal.

Satan loves rocky soil.
Sharp rocks called FEAR make that soil rocky.

Does this give you any ideas?

Are there "treasures we have buried in our heart?"

Then, finally, the Lord says to His angels, "Let's give them another chance to find their true calling and the ***"treasures we have buried in his or her hearts,"*** So the third level comes where the seed (calling) falls on thorny soil... where the thorns and the weeds grow together. It's very fertile. You say, ***"I'm going for it. I'm more determined and mature and want more out of life. I will take the risk and make something out of my life for good."***

People can survive this if they turn to God more deeply, try to understand what he's doing, and grasp the help or the resources to make it work. They keep praying and waiting on God to provide the resources they need, but most won't quit; they keep fighting.

Finally, you get to the next level—the good soil, where God says they know you're in the fertile or solid ground of your soul and have matured to fulfill your best calling.

Why are you fighting a battle already won?

Now that God has told us about the four soils our job is to identify their purpose. They may be different regarding our families, jobs, or community. Our work may be going well, but sometimes, our marriages and families are choked out by the weeds and pressures of life. We recognize what areas of our lives we need to bring to God because the lies of the enemy have taken them over. Those lies only come to kill, steal, and destroy.

I love what **Steve Jobs**, the founder of Apple, said: ***"You must love what you do (see the vision), or you will quit, like most sane people do. It's hard."***

The battle is in the mind, where the enemy will keep trying to take you off course and have you quit. I worked with one entrepreneur who went from a $2 million company to $2 billion in sales over 15 years. His vision and God's calling were so strong he would never let go. He overcame the obstacle of being raised in an orphanage and using those lessons to build teams and inspire others to reach higher.

What is God doing in your life in the midst of this?

Bob Williamson grew up in a very dark family and never heard the word love. His father beat him. His brother ridiculed him. By the time he was 14, he had an alcohol use disorder. Then he began using drugs, uppers, and downers, whatever he could get his hands on and he became a drug addict at age 17. He married and divorced at 19.

Bob tried to get into the military, but they wouldn't accept him. He was told he was incapable of love. He floated between bars, drugs, and odd jobs. He almost beat a man to death. Finally, while driving, he had a head collision. He was admitted to the hospital with a very serious injury. To keep busy while healing he was a prolific reader. His nurse, Lidia, provided library books. He kept noticing the Bible as the best-selling book of all time, and Lidia let him read her personal Bible. It was marked throughout the New Testament.

He discovered Jesus was loving, kind, and considerate to all people, but when he came to the scripture in Philippians that said, "I can do all things through Christ who strengthens me, " he got mad. He threw the Bible across the room and told the nurse the book was lying.

She said, "No, Jesus is God, he is real, and he can save your sorry ass."

He began thinking more deeply and finally, in the hospital, asked for forgiveness for his sins and gave his life to Christ. His heart changed. Thankfully, he had not killed anyone. So, when he left the hospital, he found a job at Glidden paint company, where he put labels on paint cans in Atlanta. He did so well there with a new life and a new attitude.

Glidden paint company liked his heart and business savvy and promoted him eventually to a plant manager. But he left Glidden to start and run his own business for the next 30 years. Actually, he built 13 different companies, starting in the software industry.

He sold his last businesses for $75 million and started the Jesus Alliance, among many other Christian projects.

-6-

What We Say Counts!

M**arlene Klepees** was born at only two pounds and developed Cerebral Palsy. Her parents died. She had to be in a home for paraplegics under constant care. As a teenager, she learned about Christ and gave her life to Him. She constantly dealt with evil spirits, fears, doubts, and poor nurses' care and was often unable to speak. Marlene believed she was no good to anyone. She thought of killing herself. She frequently yelled at God, asking for death or healing. Once, she even believed she was brain-dead. She could not speak. She understood but could not respond. She was often furious.

And then, Marlene had a vision of church members praying for her. So one of the nurses helped her call the church she had envisioned as she found it in the yellow pages. She then called the church and the Pastor answered.

She told him, ***"God has chosen you to pray for me***

to be healed." The Pastor was new to the church and had never prayed for anyone else for a healing miracle. However, he agreed and a van delivered her to his church. His seven-member staff joined him in prayer. He asked God to heal her from the top of her head to the bottom of her feet, and then he asked her to stand up and walk, and she did. It began with little steps and within an hour she was walking almost normally. The Pastor reminded her that he had never prayed for anyone else for a healing miracle. Today, she is a happy, healthy woman.

Does this apply to you?

Can the Prayers of Believers overcome what evil meant for bad?

Ricky Roberts has his own church True Light Ministries. He was born with a low-functioning IQ and was considered mentally retarded. His parents were distraught and constantly prayed for him. They took him to many churches and tent revivals. They persuaded Christian schools to accept him. He could barely read at the third-grade level, so University Christian School was ready to expel him by the seventh grade. Kids bullied him and called him names constantly.

His parents pleaded and pleaded for a to pray for him. In Ricky's mind, he had a sphere of doubt, rage, and anxiety in the worst way, but when a new Pastor offered to pray for him, a miracle happened. He received a healing, and today, he Pastors a church. He has five PhD's and speaks five languages. He leads spiritual healing services each Thursday in his church, and hundreds of people from throughout the city attend.

God loves the long-suffering prayers of family members and fellow believers. Never give up.

As I said, we are three-part beings: body, soul, and spirit. The body can be seen, touched, and felt. We can walk, dance, and use our bodies in many ways. The soul is the mind, will, and emotions, guided by our thoughts, words, actions, mistakes, and heartfelt desires.

In my chart, I demonstrate how the spirit is ten times bigger than the soul and even the body because it can live on earth and in heaven for eternity.

We are conceived in spirit as Jeremiah talks about ***"God knows the plans he has for us."*** (Jeremiah 29:11)

Does this apply to you?

Do some things become better when they are broken?

Is God allowing adversity?

Your soul (mind, personality, will, and emotions) works like a radio receiver. It receives evil thinking like the world that the enemy can use to twist or manipulate our thinking in the negative. Satan has the right to dial our frequency to send garbage, fearful junk (just like he did with Eve).

You can change your receiving signal station or dial and tune into the Lord's messages/scriptures, words of love, peace, and joy, the fruit of the spirit. But, until someone surrenders their heart, soul, and spirit to Christ and seeks His ways through the scripture, fellowship, and prayer for His will. Then they can start to cut off the Satan radio blasting and prevent us from receiving the complete love, peace, and joy that Christ wants for each of us.

Is God testing and refining the gold in you? The greater your call, the more challenging the obstacles the enemy will throw at you.

Yes, it's the devil, Satan, who sees his job is to destroy God's works to hate, steal, ruin, and control us. But Christ came to destroy the works of the enemy to give us love, peace, and joy, which is a fruit of the spirit, so that we can fulfill his purpose and plans in our lives.

We learn from adversity because pain draws us to him when no one else has the answers.

Our testing comes from whether we will still believe God's Word despite our circumstances being in direct opposition. Jesus was tested after God defined who He was. God tested Abraham as He did Moses, Joseph, and even King David, the "man after God's own heart" (I Samuel 13:14). We should expect to be tested as well. Testing is more than what a doctor does to assess and diagnose the problem so we can be treated and well. In the same way, God has given us the tools to diagnose and treat any adversity against us and bring down His power into the situation. We are the conduits.

People often get mad at God and wonder why He allowed bad things to happen to good people. But God will not do for us what He gives us the authority to do on our own through his guidance and leading.

He doesn't need us but chooses to work through us.

God's greatest satisfaction is leading through his children. Parents are delighted to see their children grow and mature, participate in school activities, complete homework, and compete in sports or dance. We see them grow up to be lovely people who, hopefully, continue our legacy or their legacy and the beauty of other people to build a better world.

God is a big God; He invites us to lament to Him and ask Him to use His power to make the situation right. God works through different ages. To Him, one day is like 1,000 years, so when we want the answer now, God says the answer was there two thousand years ago. He is more interested in a relationship with you than solving your problems.

Does this apply to you?

-7-

God Allows Fear to Break Our Pride

"Not everyone who says to me 'Lord, Lord,' will enter the Kingdom of Heaven, but only the one who does the will of my Father who is in heaven," Matthew 7:21.

My journey of spiritual growth began with my conversion experience. I found myself maturing spiritually through the Full Gospel Businessmen's Fellowship and the profound testimonies of fellow believers. Simultaneously, the spiritual teachings of various radio Pastors led me to attend another church. I believe it was a divine calling.

When I told my wife, she responded, ***"OK, fine, but I'm not going with you. St. Joseph's is my church. I'm not changing."*** This only deepened my resolve.

Finally, out of obedience, knowing that God was

calling me to go deeper with **Paul Zink**. I started to go to his church. He was one first Pastors I had heard on the radio. I tried to be inconspicuous and sat up on the top back row, trying to hide myself, but they were singing praise songs and people raising their hands. I was familiar with that through Full Gospel, but this Sunday, the Pastor said that the international sign was a surrender, and it was raising your hands. I immediately identified with that as a kid, watching movies of the Lone Ranger, capturing bad guys, and war stories where people held captive by the army would raise their hands and surrender.

I didn't think much of it, but on the second Sunday, in the same seat, amid praise, singing, and worship, I heard the voice of the Lord ask me, ***"Aren't you going to raise your hands?"*** while most people were singing.

I knew that was God speaking to me, and I said, ***"Lord, you know I can't do that. I might embarrass myself. I have people who would know that it's me, and I look a little loony (selfish fear from evil) since I am leading these very important high-class CEOs of companies growing with great reputations."***

But then the Holy Spirit spoke to me again and said, ***"Well, where do you think they got the signal for touchdown?"***

Immediately, I said, ***"OK, Lord, I get it! I get it."*** Football is one of my favorite pastimes, so the referee running into an end zone and raising his hands for the other team to surrender points to the other team made total sense to me; God knew how to reach me. He knew my thinking. He knows my insecurities and fears, so that was the beginning of raising my hands. Today, I enjoy raising my hands and surrendering to God during a beautiful song by the Holy Spirit. It's exciting. I enjoy it. No, I'm not crazy; it shows my belief, faith, and trust in Him.

In 1995, I knew God was calling me to sell the business. That took prayer, negotiation, and seeking the Lord over this. It was Him leading me out to sell the company. My wife did not like the idea, as she saw it as our security, but evil spirits were increasingly attacking me through various stories.

But after agreeing to the sale, the new owner wanted me to come to our annual meeting, which I had held every year in Orlando. He wanted me to introduce one of the five speakers to show continuity between us, with him taking over the business but me still having a role. The plan was that this would build confidence for the people who remained as members.

But the night before the conference, I could not sleep. Bad dreams of ***"looking stupid, being embarrassed. etc."*** kept me awake. I know that I was going through that same "junk: again, because God was shaking me loose from what I was doing, but I could not sleep, which is very unusual for me. I felt sick and went downstairs to tell the new owner. I had to go home. I felt rotten and wore a regular shirt to the breakfast table to tell him.

He said, ***"Well, you look fine to me, so get your jacket on, get over there, and do what I asked you to do—introduce the speaker!"***

I was distraught. I had already put my suitcase in my car. I stood by the car, moaning and complaining to the Lord, and finally, I said, ***"Lord, do I have to go back in there to introduce the speaker?"***

The Holy Spirit said to me, ***"Yes, go do it. It will work out fine."*** At this time, I was very uptight and nervous from a lot of ***'dirty, junk, and trash talk and thinking'*** that went through my mind: ***"You are going to embarrass yourself, look stupid, make a fool of yourself, etc."*** It was garbage coming from the enemy.

But I was obedient. I opened the trunk and got my jacket. I put on my tie. I went inside and sat down as the conference was starting. I was very, very uptight. Finally, there was a break, and now I had to go to the podium to get ready to introduce the speaker, and I was praying, ***"Lord, help me through this."*** I was still agitated and upset. The break was over. It was my turn to introduce the speaker. My knees were knocking. I was not sure that I was able to keep standing. As I opened my mouth and started to speak, the Holy Spirit came all over me, and it all went away; it was like I could fly on a cloud. I was so confident suddenly because it was the Lord working through me, and I did an excellent job introducing the speaker. I even got praise from the new owner. It was just another example of the enemy throwing trash talk at us. It taught me to trust more and pray with confidence.

Does this apply to you?

Learn How to See in the Dark

Oprah Winfrey has many stories about Christ working in her life, from her early days of a career in broadcasting business, and the difficulties of her life, as well as having been born to sharecroppers' ancestry in Mississippi. But amid enormous success, she became extremely excited to learn that the movie "The Color Purple" would be filmed and produced because she felt that acting on the big screen was one of her callings because of her heritage. The movie story was about the lives of sharecroppers in the South. She could see herself in a leading role in the movie even though she was not an actress and had no training. She was outspoken, a good communicator, and likable to all audiences. So, she sent a letter to Steven Spielberg, the producer, asking if she could have an audition to play a leading role.

For months, she heard nothing, but she loved and sang the song "I Surrender All." Then, on one of her shows, her guest was country singer Faith Hill, and she asked Faith to sing that song. Oprah shared her passion and struggle with wanting to be in the movie but had no response to her request for an audition for months. She had become frustrated. She had thoughts and guilt feelings that ***"I am too fat, they don't want me, I am never going to make it. You must be stupid ever to consider you could be an actress and play the leading role."*** These thoughts kept ringing in her mind.

So, she decided to go to a fat farm for a week—go on a diet, exercise, jog, and do all the things her coach told her to do. But while she was jogging, this song came over and over in her heart: ***"I surrender all."*** Every day. In her words, she had a spiritual encounter where she surrendered her life to Christ again. She said, ***"God, do with me what you want; I surrender all to you."***

Oprah was jogging and singing when a lady from the clubhouse stopped her on the track and said, ***"Oprah, there's an important phone call for you. It's from a man named Steven."***

She left to take the call, and Steven Spielberg said, ***"I heard you're at a fat farm."***

She said, ***"No, sir. I'm just jogging."***

He said, ***"I don't want you to lose one ounce of***

weight. I'm auditioning you for the lead role in 'The Color Purple'... Don't change a thing. You're just what I need."

Can you see it? It's another example of how the enemy can twist our thinking and create worry, doubts, and fears, but God's purpose is for us to trust him more and more. ***"He knows the plans that he has for you."***

Have you thought about the plans God has for you?

Do You and I lack patience?

I heard a famous woman say in a teaching, "The Lord is wonderful and full of love, kindness, and fruitfulness, but he is just too slow for me."

What do you think? I agree. Obviously, he is spinning the world faster, with technology, cell phones, Zoom meetings, and the world coming together to do business in just hours across the Continents. Costco wants blueberries year-round in its stores. So, **Family Tree Farms** and **Driscoll's** for example, are farming on seven continents, so we eat less processed foods to live healthier.

Jack Manilla probably agrees, too. He grew up in Pennsylvania, worked his way through college, worked for a large company for years, and eventually came south to take a vice president role in a mid-size business. However, he had a significant conflict with his boss, who was very egotistical and had lied to him on various occasions.

Finally, Jack, a man of character, resigned without a job. He had to sell his house, boat, and cars because he was overextended financially. His son, who worked in New York City, had a little pink house in central Florida that he would allow him and his mother to live in. So, Jack, being a good Catholic and hardworking man, sought another corporate job. After fifteen interviews, he had no offers. He prayed, ***"Lord, help me find the right job. I'm only in my 50's. I want to still be successful in another business or enterprise."*** So, he walked deeper and deeper into the orange groves next to his home each day, praying and asking God louder and louder to send him a job. He studied his Bible each day.

A good friend recommended that there was a pool company for sale in Jacksonville, Florida. He told his friend no thank you but that he knew nothing about building swimming pools. Finally, his friend convinced him to meet with the owner, who was going to retire. The owner said. ***"I want to sell you my business,"*** Jack said, ***"I have no money or experience in the pool business."***

The owner said, ***"OK, I'm going to take you to the bank, and I will borrow the money I want for the price***

of the business. You will pay me back as you pay off the bank loan."

Of course, Jack had 25 different fears and doubts from the enemy come through his mind, i.e., ***"I'm not qualified. I do not know the pool business. I don't even own a swimming pool or know the construction business."***

"God help me. I don't know what I am doing," was his cry. Since suddenly, he was an owner, he started to roll up his sleeves and get busy. But within a year, he learned that instead of building pools, it was easier and better cash flow to maintain pools for wealthy individuals, clubs, and hotels.

After training and licensing, he became an expert in the field and a leading authority. Cruise ships hired him from the Mediterranean to East Asia to help them with the chemical balance in the pools.

He became president of the **National Pool Owners Association**. His peers asked for his expertise.

This is just another example of what God can do if we let go and let him take over. He will give us visions, understanding, and wisdom for the places he wants to take us.

So don't believe everything you think.

Does this apply to you?

Does He See Beauty in Your Scars?

While God sent Jesus to break Satan's power, He wants us to surrender and trust Him and take the authority to keep Satan out of our thoughts and lives. But we must exercise that power. In my early years with Christ, I failed to be in His Word each day and allow it to be embodied. I would be fearful and hear: ***"You are going to look so stupid!" "Who is going to believe you?" "What makes you qualified to teach others?"***

In the book of James, we learn that there are two kinds of wisdom in the world. To paraphrase. ***"Your worldly wisdom, that which does not come from heaven, but harbors bitterness, and selfishness, and is unspiritual leads to evil practice. But the wisdom that comes from heaven is pure, peace-loving, considerate, full of mercy, good fruit, sincerity, and a harvest of righteousness."***

2 Corinthians 10:3-5 tells us, "*We live in a world where we do not wage war as the world does.*"

There is a double life for every Christian. We must be in the world but not live as the world does. The weapons we fight with are not the weapons of the world. On the contrary, they have divine power to demolish every pretense against the Kingdom of God.

Therefore we must,
take captive every thought to the obedience of God.

Again, God and Christ are the Word. God embodies words. The Lord says the battle is not yours but mine. God is giving us the authority.

— Luke 10:19 —

"again, all authority is given to you to trample
on snakes and scorpions, in the end,
overcome all the power of the end of
the enemy, nothing will harm you."

Does this give you any ideas?

-8-

Trash Talk or Junk Food

You don't have to see demons to experience their fear or remind you of past failures, torturous memories from childhood, or even when a teacher said you were stupid.

Demons can enter and possess unbelievers; they cannot enter the body of those who belong to the Lord. Satan and demons are defeated foes, yet they are still very active in this world, twisting our thinking and causing much harm. Though they cannot possess and control a believer, they can cause problems. It's our responsibility to recognize the attacks and command them to go in Jesus' Name.

— *James 4:7* —

"Submit yourselves therefore to God. Resist the devil, and he will flee from you,"

Evil brings up what I call Trash talk or Junk food. It's how the enemy is trying to squash what God wants from us. But the Lord wants to use His loving callings to help move the world forward and overcome evil. When we speak, we carry the power God has given us authority to be in charge of our lives.

— Deuteronomy 30:16 —

"Choose this day, life or
death blessings, or curses.

— Proverbs 18:21 —

"the tongue has the power of life and death."

— Ephesians 4:29 —

We are to put a guard over our mouths
and let no corruption communication
proceed out of our mouths.

Again, that's why the Lord says don't believe everything you think. If you think garbage is coming from God, you are wrong. Garbage is coming from the enemy to try to take you down and separate you from God, give you sure doubt, earth distrust, why are you to live in confusion.

"If Satan can't make you bad,
he will make you busy."
— Anonymous

Should you pray more?

-9-

Be Not Double Minded

Unbelief causes double-mindedness and confusion so that someone can't decide what they believe concerning a matter. The definition of a double-minded person is ***"having opposite or opposing views at different times in the mind."*** These people can be living in fear or uncertain of their real calling. They move on to what is urgent. A business analogy could be whether a leader is Working "ON" the business or "IN" the business. Working IN the business focuses just on daily activities that need to be done. However, working "ON" the business is working at least 20% of the time on its future success. Marketing Strategic Initiatives vs. Daily Tactics and Activities can lead to constant fighting off fires.

But if you have no growth, you will ultimately die or suffer more. Someone described it as ***"spiritual ignorance***

or schizophrenic." A further definition of that would be a divided interest, between God and the world.

— James 1:7-9 —

"That person should not expect to receive
anything from the Lord. 8 Such a person
is double-minded and unstable in all they do."

— James 4:8 —

"Come near to God, and he will come near
to you. Wash your hands, sinners, and
purify your hearts, you double-minded."

What does this mean? Unfortunately, most people who say they are Christians go to church regularly, but they are not sold out to God. They are comfortable in their lifestyle, and if God said, ***"I want you to give $10,000 to your neighbor or missionaries to Africa,"*** they would disregard it and call it a crazy thought.

I just spoke with a woman who told me about the conflicts and difficulties in her life. And while she attends church regularly, she is not a bit dependent on the Lord for guidance or directions or better circumstances.

She shared how she often feels lost and uncertain, despite her regular church attendance, and how she longs for a deeper connection with God.

She has no sense of her calling.

— Romans 12:2 —

"Do not be conformed to this world, but be transformed by the renewing of your mind, that by testing you may discern what is the will of God, what is good and acceptable and perfect."

A simple way to paraphrase that scripture is ***"be not of the world when you are in the world."*** If you are not committed to Christ, you are not in His will but your own. Doubt should not rule your heart; you cannot serve two masters. You cannot serve God and the enemy at the same time. Your thinking is just lukewarm in your faith. As described in the Bible, lukewarm faith is a state of spiritual indifference or apathy, where one's commitment to God is half-hearted. Either God is in control or not.

God seeks people willing to change, take risks, be obedient, and sacrifice. God wants single-minded people. The more you praise God in good times and bad, the more fruitful, exciting, and rewarding your life will be. The Lord wants to meet you in Heaven and say, "***Well done, thy good and faithful servant.***"

-10-

The World's Way — Bad News Sells

Early in our marriage, my wife and I came back from the Peace Corps, and I worked at the Ann Arbor, Michigan, Chamber of Commerce. This was a good experience. My assignment was downtown, so I met officers at the police department. Each time I visited, I noticed the same reporters from television stations with a camera guy and a reporter for the newspaper. What I realized was they were waiting there to find out the most shocking, worst stories they could tell and who got arrested, who shot who, and who murdered for Frontline front-page news for TV stations and the newspapers.

The old phrase ***"bad news sells"*** unfortunately is true in our society where evil reigns in many ways.

For instance, it's no wonder that murder, robbery, and all manner of sin, along with adverse weather conditions, dominate today's headlines. It would be a breath of fresh air to hear that ***'New Governor Tom Jones has dedicated his life to Christ and pledges to love his enemies, bringing the Bible back into our schools.'***

In the 1950s, attorneys could not advertise. The Media could not show nudity. Why? They are harmful to our Christian society established by our Founding Fathers. ***Today, it's about the world's way and greed. It's not about love but fear.***

Today, Pharmaceutical drugs are the leading television and evening news sponsors. Do you hurt somewhere? See your doctor. So, in the United States, unfortunately, our Health Care System is no longer about health but about wealth. Big Pharma reigns, and they control the FDA. The word Pharmacia comes from the Greek word poisons and strongholds. Only the USA and New Zealand allow advertisement of pharmaceutical drugs on television. Our processed food diet is another significant contributor to the United States leading the world in heart and cancer deaths.

Bad news sells, ***"go see your doctor if you have these symptoms."*** It causes people to fear, doubt, and worry about going to a doctor, while it produces more income, and pressures news outlets to be reluctant to report good news. It all works against faith, love, peace, and joy—the fruit of the Spirit. It is a highly negative and destructive response to what God wants us to do by getting us into His word. The Lord wants a society of good news, encouragement, and trusting in him.

Only God can turn a MESS into a message,

a TEST into a Testimony, a trial a Triumph,

and a VICTIM into a victory

What is your mess that can become a message?

-11-

How Obedient Can You Be

Who would you risk prison to share Christ with?

B**ud Toole**, a good friend, was a senior VP of a major insurance company and oversaw their investment portfolio. Bud and his wife, Carolyn, went to an Executive Dinner, and he gave his life to Christ. Then, they joined with five other couples to start a church, which today is a dynamic organization with 4,000 members and 35 outreach ministries.

In the 1980s, Bud's friend, **John Maisel**, invited him to go to Russia at the height of Communism. Despite the risks, Bud led a group of men who eagerly accepted the invitation. One of them had a Russian friend who asked him to bring some Bibles. At the last minute, Bud discovered that he was smuggling at least six Bibles in his coat and suitcase. At that time, security was not that strong, but the mission was not without danger.

Yet, it was dangerous when they met with small groups of Russians in their homes for prayer and Bible reading. They ensured all curtains were closed because the KGB would watch on the streets and ensure lights were off by 10 p.m. Twice a year, he would return with other believers to help the Russian people learn to believe, pray, and study the Word.

Twice, he was arrested, but through a miracle, he was interrogated but not imprisoned while still a VP of a major company. That was a significant risk. But in 1989, the Iron Curtain came down, and the doors opened rapidly so believers could travel more freely and spread the Word to those hungry for Christ. John and Bud founded East-West Ministries. Bud spent at least seven years in Austria, spearheading their efforts in Eastern Europe and Russia. Today, East-West is working in 40 different countries.

The Bible has much to say about obedience. Obedience is an essential part of the Christian faith. Jesus Himself was ***"obedient unto death, even death on a cross"*** Philippians 2:8. The definition of obedience is ***"dutiful or submissive compliance to the commands of one in authority."*** But it is important to remember that our obedience to God is not solely a matter of duty. We obey Him because we love Him, and His love for us is boundless and unconditional, making us feel loved and cherished.

Does this apply to you?

— John 14:23 —

23 Jesus replied, "Anyone who loves me will obey my teaching. My father will love them, and we will come to them and make our home with them.

Ed Kobel, CEO of DeBartolo Development, runs a large Real Estate Development firm founded by his father, who was the first to develop indoor malls in America. Ed got involved as a CEO in a roundtable group led by **Henry Blackaby** and became the author of the famous workbook, ***Experiencing God***. Henry urged the CEOs of large companies to pray before they got to the office to ask God what the priorities for the day were, most of them rejected the idea because they said, ***"You don't realize how busy we are; how many appointments we have a day, etc."*** but Ed decided to try it. He would pray in the morning, asking God what his priorities would be that day, and then listen.

You can imagine the interference he would receive from the enemy trying to tell him, ***"What a stupid idea! Do you think God is going to talk to you? You think he even cares about you and especially your business?"*** But instead, it worked for Ed, drawing him closer to making better decisions.

Then, one day a year later, the Lord told Ed to ***"Sell the majority of your 2 1/2 billion dollars' worth of real estate. A downturn in the economy is coming."***

Ed was surprised, but after nearly a year of researching the idea, he realized that a correction or recession in the marketplace could shut down development.

Finally, he told his board that he thought it was time to sell their significant assets and buy them back later when the economy started to grow again. They laughed and asked who told him that. When he said, ***"The Lord,"*** they laughed louder. They said it was a crazy idea because they were making more money now than ever.

Ed's unwavering faith and trust in God's guidance were not in vain. They sold most of their properties, and the economy crashed as predicted.

Two or three years later, the Lord led them to buy back the properties. This time, they were able to purchase them at less than half the original price, effectively doubling their assets to nearly $5 billion. This success story is a testament to the transformative power of faith and the rewards it can bring, instilling hope and optimism in the hearts of the readers.

Can God talk to you that way, too?

You'll have to get through the maze of junk the enemy will try to throw at you.

-12-

The Power of Reprogramming Faith

Every believer will come to a time when they need to reset their faith. It does not matter how long they have been walking with the Lord because the tests of life happen to all of us.

— John 16:33 —

"I have told you these things so that in me you may have peace. In this world, you will have trouble. But take heart! I have overcome the world,"

Instead of saying, I'm afraid, or I don't know, be open to declaring, ***"God is healing me. I have been overcoming my fears through my faith in Christ. He is my rock, Satan. You have no territory right here over me. My rights come from Christ; be gone Satan, in the name of Jesus."***

— *Roman 10:17* —

So, faith comes from hearing, that is, hearing the Good WORD and teachings of Christ.

As we continue to repeat this, we are all reprogramming our soul or mind. While doubts may still exist, our personalities, will, and emotions will grow confidently with dependence on Christ.

Reprogramming

In other words, your soul will reprogram itself into the word and leading of God to live in you into your soul and take over the negative thinking or the fears or doubts.

Said another way, verbal expression is the catalyst that speeds mental acceptance. If I say something often enough and my negative soul hears it, the mind starts to say: we need to reprogram. "He's changed his thinking and our database." This is a call to action, a reminder of the power we hold in our words.

Hearing in your soul, the soul starts replacing old thinking with new in your mind, as it rings in your ears often enough to change your attitudes and actions.

When we were first married, my wife, Judy, and I had a common heart to serve others. We went into the Peace Corps for two years in Brazil, where we lived and volunteered to help in favela/slum areas. For three months before we left, we went through training, including six hours a day of speaking Portuguese, not reading, and only talking, repeating, and learning the sounds of the words and phrases. During the first two months, we never received a book. We just spent time memorizing and repeating phrases. We started with simple stuff, such as ***"How are you? What is your name, etc.?"*** We were memorizing, repeating, and getting Portuguese into our souls, heads, and hearts. It was tough for us. But that is what God wants from us—to memorize and repeat scripture into our souls and hearts.

After a year in Brazil, I could think in Portuguese and did not have to translate. The Lord wants you and I to believe in the Holy Spirit in His Word/His heart. Yes, you still must know how to do things in the world. "Be in the World, but not of the World but of Christ." You must be Bi-Lingual, meaning you need to be fluent in the language of the world and the language of Christ. Just as being bilingual in a worldly sense opens more opportunities, being bilingual in faith allows you to navigate the world while staying true to your Christian values.

So, every morning, I quote powerful verses from Ephesians saying, ***"I put on the armor of God, my life is resurrected, with unspeakable joy, that surpasses all understanding. I put on the helmet of salvation, the breastplate of righteousness girds up with the loins of truth, shod with the preparation of the gospel of peace, and giving a shield of faith in Christ, which quenches***

the fiery darts of the enemy. The word of God is stronger than a double-edged sword, and it separates bone from marrow, soul from spirit. It judges the attitudes and the thoughts of the heart and the soul in the name of Jesus Christ." *(Ephesians 6:10-18)*

A double-edged sword can cut through both physical and spiritual objects.

Should you pray more?

-13-

Stink Like Jesus

Evil hates the Word of God when we speak or take it in. When we live in His Word, we praise the Lord. He flees. God embodies his Word. The enemy can't penetrate our shield. It's the aroma of God and His incense. ***The scent of God on us keeps evil away.***

- ✓ A skunk lets out a terrible odor when it feels like it will be attacked or harmed. Very few people can withstand its odor and run.
- ✓ Even bears cannot withstand the pungent odor of pine sol, apple cider vinegar, Lysol, Neem oil, or rubbing alcohol. They will run from it.
- ✓ My wife and I live on a property that backs up to a 100 acre preserve. Unfortunately, deer like our shrubs in their diet. So we have learned to plant garlic plants at our lot line. Deer don't like garlic smell so they stay away.

- ✓ As humans we are driven away from smoke, gasoline smells, dead fish, and many more.
- ✓ Let me repeat, when we live in His Word and we praise the Lord. Evil flees. We stink!

A quick reminder

— 1 Corinthians 2:14 —

"The person without the Spirit does not accept the things that come from the Spirit of God but considers them foolish and cannot understand them because they are discerned only through the Spirit. The person with the Spirit makes judgments about all things, However, such a person is not subject to merely human judgments."

— 2 Corinthians 2:14-15—

"But thanks be to God, who always leads us as captives in Christ's triumphal procession and uses us to spread the aroma of the knowledge of him everywhere. For we are to God the pleasing aroma of Christ among those who are being saved and those who are perishing."

So, we Stink to Satan!!

You have heard me say that Satan has tried to come against me again and again in hotel rooms, speaking before an audience with negative thoughts and fears. His messages are always to remind me: ***"You're going to look stupid. You're going to embarrass yourself. You're not smart enough; No one will believe you. Don't make a fool of yourself."***

It was my pride to be in control.
God wants me to trust Him.

Live in Him, Abide in Him

The enemy is trying to keep us from pursuing God and the more profound thoughts of life and calling.

Yes, he would like to see you commit suicide or spread hate in every way you can.

Is it overcoming Toxic Charity?

Jeff Rutt grew up on a dairy farm, where he learned hard work and discipline until his mom left the family, which caused him great pain and suffering. As a youth, he turned to Christ and as a dedicated Christian, he and his wife eventually sold the farm and started a home building business near Lancaster, Pennsylvania. Today, the business is successful, producing as many as 400 new homes a year.

However, as his church saw the crisis in Eastern Europe after the fall of communism in 1989, they felt the heart to help people in Ukraine with food and supplies. He traveled there with humanitarian supplies of food and clothing. However, within a year, they learned from a Ukrainian Pastor and merchant that their help was making people dependent on their supplies, so churches and local merchants were hurting by their giving. It has been called "Toxic Charity." So, after much prayer, Jeff Rutt started Hope International providing people the opportunity to begin their own business for self-employment through microfinacing. They have raised over a billion dollars. Over 95% of loans are repaid, and borrowers learn about Christ in small groups. They operate in 22 countries. Hundreds of thousands have come to Christ through huddle meetings and teachings each month.

Does this apply to you?

-14-

God is the Giver of Visions.

Perhaps God is giving you a vision for a future where you go back to school or start a new career. Or perhaps God is giving you a picture of a ministry he wants you to start one day. These things in life always start with an idea, a dream, a vision, or hope. When God wants something for us in the future, he often puts a vision in our minds for this outcome in the present, so we know what to work toward.

God's visions are not exclusive. They are for everyone. In Genesis 1:28, ***God's nature is revealed as that of a visionary and creator.*** He gives visions to inventors, lovers of people, mothers, fathers, business leaders, and even kids. His visions are for all of us.

Listen to the stories of these visionaries.

As a young boy, **Steven Spielberg's** father said he

would take him to a circus. He was so excited as his father described what went on with the different animals and entertainment, but when he got there, it was not a circus, but a movie about a circus, by **Cecil B. DeMille**. Nevertheless, he became very enchanted and saw the vision of doing this one day. As a 10-year-old, using his mother's little movie camera, he created his first film about friends at camp. His parents loved and encouraged Steven during crisis and tough times.

God has chosen certain people to receive a vision from Him of how they can change the lives of others around them; I wrote about it in my book, ***The Untold Secret that Creates True Wealth***, where I discussed the parable of the sower as recorded in Mathew, Luke, and Mark. It's not about money, but it is about changing hearts and influencing people for God's greatest purposes. Steven could have quit many times, but he didn't. He became the top movie producer in the history of our country, producing some of the most famous movies ever made. As you read these stories, consider whether God's vision applies to you.

Are you ready to embrace the vision he has for your life?

-15-

Overcoming My Pride Again.

The word pride can be found 55 times in the Bible. It is undue confidence in and attention to one's skills, accomplishments, state, possessions, or position. Pride is easier to recognize than define and more straightforward to identify in others than oneself. Additionally, many words describe this concept, each with its emphasis. Synonyms for pride include arrogance, presumption, conceit, self-satisfaction, boasting, and high-mindedness. It is the opposite of humility, the proper attitude one should have about God. Pride is rebellion against God because it attributes to oneself the honor and glory due to God alone.

Hurricane Andrew was a devastating storm ready to hit Miami head-on in August 1992. Everyone in Florida was concerned because it could hurt our whole state. Praying became important—not just in church, but even in the media. Fortunately, the Lord intervened, and at the last minute, it diverted further south into the less populated area of Homestead on Florida's lower east coast. The wreckage was enormous. Families and businesses reached out to help. I felt like the Lord was urging me to help the Homestead Chamber. So, we organized a workshop series where four top speakers agreed to speak for free and covered their travel and hotel expenses. The goal was to raise $10-20,000 to help the Chamber. I flew down there the night before and had dinner with the speakers to share the next day.

Again, I felt enormous evil pressure saying you are going to "look stupid, you are a failure" while leading the meeting. It was so deep that I almost cried. I knelt on the side of my bed. As I prayed, I felt enormous pressure all around me and incredible pain and agony, and I yelled out, ***"Lord, I can't take this. I can't take this. I give up!! I give up!!"*** I yelled twice, and within moments. I said, ***"Lord, I can't do this. The pressure is too great! I give up!"***

The Holy Spirit then spoke to me and said. ***"GOOD...I have been waiting for you to say that!! Let Me do it through you. Why are you accepting the pressure from the enemy? Let go of your pride, and let me lead you. I will take over from here."***

"Everything will be fine tomorrow. You will enjoy the day, and I am in control."

Wow!! Peace came all over me, and it was an incredible experience. I felt tremendous PEACE. All fear went away. It was like I could fly on the wings of an eagle. I was so confident suddenly because the Lord was working through me. I did a fine job introducing he speakers and even got some praise. It was another example of how the enemy will throw trash talk at you: Like "***you're not good enough; you're never going to make it.***" Evil was sending FEAR. Trying to keep us from God's ultimate plan. God was repeatedly teaching me to trust Him more profoundly and deeply. It's a hard way to learn.

I slept through the night like a baby. That morning, I got up feeling like I was flying on the wings of an eagle. Things went very smoothly: the introductions and speakers were great, as were the breakout sessions. There was activity and fun for the attendees, and we gave the Chamber of Commerce a nice-sized check.

This is another example of me trying to control things but slowly learning to give up. How about you? Do you have the same problem I did? The Lord repeatedly taught me to allow Him to be in control—a HARD way to learn.

God has a calling for each of our lives.

Satan knows the calling God has for your life. He desires to keep you in the "in the dark" as long as possible, filled with "junk food" or "trash talk" from the World or media sound bites filled with worry and doubt. He wants to keep you worried about media junk and wishes to visit your doctor for answers rather than seeking the Lord for peace, love, and joy.

Your Calling vs. the Battle

Levels of your calling	*Levels of the battle*
• Faithful Servant	• High Pressure
• Friend	• Fear
• Disciple	• Selfishness
• Teacher	• Afraid
• Leader	• Doubtful
• Inferior	• Full of Doubt High
• Visionary	• Deceit

We have all heard how the natural pressure of a diamond turns it into a beautiful object that women cherish.

I loved it when **Jon Heyman**, author of ***Agonizing Peace***, talked about his testimony of being born in Greece and abandoned in an orphanage in Athens. He never met his parents or truly knew his date of birth. However, when he was six years old, an American adopted him and brought him to the States, and he eventually became a leader of children and teenage ministries serving Christ. He said, ***"Pressure is good. A basketball is no good without the right air pressure. That is what I needed to battle and***

mature in my Christ calling. It made me stronger and a better leader."

Pat Morley had a rough upbringing because his mom left him, his father, and his four brothers. Remarkably, his father persevered and kept them in church. Then, as a young man, he left school to join the military. Drunk one night, he drove off the side of the road and was so upset and shaken he dedicated his life to making a difference and being a man of influence. He got his GED and entered the Commercial Real Estate business in Florida. He got his master's degree and became one of Central Florida's top developers.

As a dedicated Christian, he served the Lord by helping men overcome many of the struggles he had faced.

His first book, ***Man in Mirror, solving 24 Problems Men Face,*** which sold 4 million copies, became a foundation for his ministry, helping men face their toughest challenges. Today, ***Man in the Mirror*** is helping 35,000 Churches with millions of men reached. Today, Pat continues to write and is working on his 24th book and message.

Evil Repellents: Can we stink?

I searched the Bible and the teachings of ***Prayers that Avail Much*** by **Germaine Copeland** for ways to overcome the enemy. I have prayed for at least 30 years, and I am learning to call it my "Satan or Evil Repellent."

— *Ephesians 6:10* —

"I put on the armor of God, the helmet of salvation, and the breastplate of righteousness girds up with the lounges of Truth, shod with the preparation of the gospel of peace, given the shield of faith that quenches the fiery darts of the enemy, and the sword of the spirit, which is the Word of God. The Word of God is stronger than a double-edged sword, separating bone from morrow, soul from spirit. It judges the attitudes of the heart and soul in the name of Jesus, amen."

Back to the beginning of this book.
What are your thoughts?

In 2 Corinthians 13: 5 we read: ***"Examine yourself to see whether you are in faith. Test yourselves. Do you not realize this about yourselves, that Jesus Christ is in you, unless, of course, you fail to meet the test?"***

This statement gives all Christians a crucial perspective on looking inward. We assess ourselves to see any skepticism and be honest and careful while looking into our lives. It is an invitation to be honest about your walk with the Lord and use this to correct anything out of alignment.

Should you seek Wise Counsel?

-16-

Adopted for Success?

Pat Kelly's mother could not manage her two boys when their father developed an alcohol use disorder. She struggled to lose her home, so she put her two boys in the Virginia Home for Boys, an orphanage near Richmond.

Along with **Bill Riddell**, Pat started Physician Sales & Service (PSS), which supplied doctors' offices medical supplies. I met them when they were doing $2 million in sales in Jacksonville and Tampa. Pat, the CEO, told me his passion to become a $500 million business in 10 years. He was bright, likable, and a go-getter in so many ways. I got him involved in the CEO roundtable of TEC when most companies were doing $65 million in sales and were not sure they wanted him involved. But he was a sponge and loved to learn and apply what he knew.

Pat was one of two of our TEC members who won the Horatio Alger Award for outstanding entrepreneur leaders who joined the ***"from rags to riches"*** legends honored by the Horatio Alger Association.

When Pat and I got together at lunch occasionally, I would pray over the food. He thought I was a little crazy. He said he didn't think God cared about him because he spent his childhood in an orphanage. He had no mother or father. ***(Evil will give us "feelings of abandonment" and make us believe we are no good).*** But I would remind Pat that one of his secrets to success was how he developed teams, shared numbers, profitability, and so many of the ***'sharing principles'*** he learned in the orphanage.

Even when the economy went through a downturn, and Pat had to make tough decisions like cutting wages, he remained committed to his employees. He promised to share stock ownership, a testament to his belief in the power of shared success.

Pat also learned from one of our top speakers, **Jack Stack**, who authored ***Great Game of Business***, and pioneered ***"Open Book Management,"*** a strategy that drove teamwork and profitability. In the orphanage, Pat learned how to share and build teams. Some of the same principles Jack was teaching, Pat had learned in the orphanage. His journey is a powerful reminder that God allows us to learn from painful experiences for a greater purpose and a bigger calling. Pat, who found faith later in life, generously gave back to the Virginia Home for Boys, the place that had once been his refuge.

Should you pray more?

-17-

The Unseen Dirty Work of the Enemy

Too many Christians don't understand or have never been taught that we are in a war. Satan or the devil wants to destroy all the works of the Lord. It's his mission to keep an ignorant, self-centered nature in our weak logic. That is what I addressed in the early part of this book. The doubts, fear, ***"stinking thinking"*** about yourself or lack of confidence do not come from God but evil's way of limiting our effectiveness. God allows it to mold us into stronger and more effective ways of using his ways and overcoming evil.

However, there are experiences where I had difficulty, and I share them because I have learned from them. As the expression goes, these are ***"the tip of the iceberg."*** I am not an expert in this field, but I believe it is essential to address and expose more of it to all of us. Hopefully, my true stories will give you a deeper understanding of something that might impact you or friends that you should research more.

Strongholds are demonic or negative influences that continue to grip a person's thinking, bad habits, or actions.

Curses or spells are verbal condemnations placed on people that Satan can use against someone.

Sins of the Father could be strongholds, curses, and evil habits inherited from our ancestors. Just like we inherit physical and personality traits from our parents, we can inherit spiritual traits and sins from our parents. Some of these can be broken once someone submits their life to Christ. Others can continue until the Holy Spirit brings them to our attention. I feel called to share and bring more to your attention.

Unforgiveness. You cannot be alive and not experience this. We all have been offended or hurt by someone. Not all are on purpose, and there are examples of the issue being our pride. The incredible part is that Jesus died on the cross to forgive everyone's sins. Satan tries to keep us caught in our prideful state of thinking we are OK, except for the trash talk he keeps reminding us of.

The Lord God has been frustrated with His children for centuries because of our ignorance and mistakes. He loves us and wants the best for us, just like we want for our kids. Jesus came to forgive us by dying on the cross.

He brought GRACE that so many do not see the Spiritual life Christ wants from each of us. I will explain more and why in Chapter 23 ***'Christian Religion vs, Relationship.'*** A significant probability is the stinking thinking Satan is putting into our mind. We settle for average. But if we praise Christ often, He will reveal more to us. He embodies forgiveness, love, praise and passion.

What areas do you want to explore?

Breaking Strongholds

Guy Iannello got involved with drugs as a teenager in upstate New York. He thought of himself as a successful entrepreneur with guns and limo drivers. He came to Florida to continue his habit and business and met a beautiful woman he convinced to marry him. His company got dangerous with drug arrests, but somehow, he was not sentenced to prison. He promised his wife he would give it up but couldn't kick the habit, so she left him. People had witnessed to him about Christ and urged him to surrender. Finally, he went to church with a friend, and the Pastor taught him about the changed life by following Christ.

He went home that day, broke down and cried as he surrendered his life to Christ. But as he opened his eyes, his dog barked violently in terror at a huge snake. He cried out, ***"Oh Lord, help me. What is that?"***

The Lord spoke to him audibly and said, "***This is the serpent I just cast out of you.***"

Guy was inspired as he studied the Word and became a teacher. His marriage was restored. With his wife, he oversees a ministry to teach the Word and help addicts and alcoholics. They go into jails and encourage the prisoners to learn and memorize the Word of God for life-changing and inner healing. It's a compelling program, and I have sent people to him and had him speak for us in Wise Counsel.

Does this apply to you?

David Hairabedian's Jewish father was a Hi-Dive champion, pushing him to be a winner and excel at whatever he did. But in college, he found that selling drugs paid him more than part-time jobs. So, at 20 years old, he got caught in a drug trafficking scheme stealing a private jet. His next challenge was in a Leavenworth Penitentiary cell. One day, Jesus miraculously appeared before him, transforming his life to prepare him for miracles during his 20-year sentence. Then, the Lord led him to a healing ministry for fellow prisoners that rocked the inmates.

Today, he and his beautiful wife, Joanna, have a ministry to African prisons (giving away 10,000 leather-bound Bibles). They have authored 15 books, including ***Jet Ride to Hell*** and ***Journey to Freedom***, and have delivered hundreds from strongholds by their prayers asking for cleansing. They are founders of VitualChurchMedia.com.

Sexual Curses

The **Christian Healing Ministry** has found that 25% of young girls have been molested sexually by family members or others. In fact 20% of young boys have had the same experience. This leaves a scar and hook for Evil to torment men and women. It can drive them away from sex in great fear or create an abnormal craving for sex with anyone willing or even rape. Pornorgraphy can fuel the appetite or lead to prostitution or ruined marriages. It can be one of the sins of the Father or Mother passed on through their children. "Sins of father can last for six generations." Both the soul and Spirit are impacted. Forgiveness and healing prayer can break the curse with intercessors.

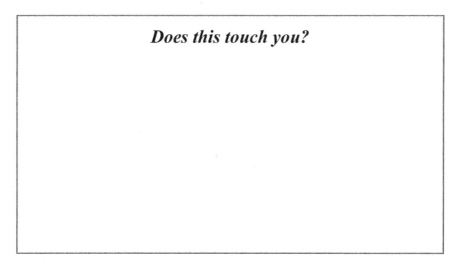

Does this touch you?

Sins of my father

When I was a teenager, my father came home from his train commute from downtown Chicago exhausted and probably from a tough day. But he was just in time for dinner. I said something disrespectful or smart-alecky. It took him no time to show his temper, which was very quick. You never knew when it would happen. He told me to go to my bedroom, yelling at me. In my room, I locked the door and lay on my bed. He came to my door, yelling at me and trying to break down the door with his shoulder. I got up and let him in. Very mad; he yelled at me to pull my pants down and whipped me. Then he said as he always did, ***"You're lucky I don't use a belt like my father did."***

When he left, I cried on that bed and ***"swore I would never lose my temper to my kids."***

Years later, with four kids and a recent commitment to Christ, I began to pray before dinner. As I did, my second daughter, as a teenager, started to mouth off in an ugly way. I told her to go to her room. But all down the hall, she was yelling back at me. So, I did the usual thing: I followed her to her room. She yelled at me, saying, ***"Would Jesus lose his temper?"*** I said ***"yes,"*** thinking of the moneychangers in the Temple. I did not spank her, but grabbed her wrist to slow her down, and then my backhand hit the dresser next to her bed; the pain was enormous as I returned to the kitchen table.

The Lord used that experience to teach me that I had inherited the same quick temper as my dad. The Bible says the sins of the father are passed down for five or six generations. These are known as strongholds. The back of my hand stayed swollen for a year. So, hundreds of times, I asked the Lord for forgiveness, which removed and broke my quick temper and the sins of my father. I have been very thankful for that experience and what I learned. It helped to make me a better person.

Revelation—I now see how God has been teaching me in His English. His Words are the language I need to think and speak. As I have said, God is His Word, Love, Peace, and Joy. I abide in Him, and He abides in me.

Does this give you ideas?

Curses

Bill and Mary are a highly successful couple who work in financial planning and invest money for many successful clients. They were both touched by their participation in learning, helping, and praying for individuals and families through the Christian Healing Ministry, an international group with over 500 trained intercessors worldwide.

Out of compassion, they allowed two teenage boys from Afghanistan to live with them during high school. The boys' mother encouraged them to do so as she did not have room for them in her home.

One day, Mary got sick and could not get out of bed. Her husband and others prayed for her, but it got worse. Finally, one day, someone suggested she may have been "cursed." Friends prayed to break the curse. She returned to her normal good health.

But Bill asked the two boys, ***"Did they know anything about curses?"***

They said, ***"Of course, our mother puts curses on people all the time in Islam."***

Does this apply to you or someone you know?

My Curse?

When I was four, I fell off my tricycle and landed on my face. I knocked out all four of my front teeth.

My mom and dad later thought it was funny. So, when friends came by, my mom always said, ***"Johnny, show them your smile."*** So, with no front teeth, everyone laughed. I felt ashamed.

When the next teeth came in, they were not in order, so I had braces; then, I got hit in the mouth with a baseball bat and fell at the swimming pool, breaking my other front tooth. Then they got smashed in football practice. So, they stuck a titanium pin in one tooth, which I discovered as an adult was leaking metal into my brain cells.

The problems have not stopped, but I believe the Lord

has shown me that my parents unknowingly were cursing me—every time I was embarrassed as a kid, God is still in the business of healing and removing curses.

So, where do negative thoughts most often come from? Yes, evil and our enemies, drawing on our past or inherited experiences!

Does this apply to you?

Overcoming the curse of poverty

Millard Fuller was a bright attorney and businessman in Alabama who worked so hard that his wife called him a "workaholic" because sometimes he slept in his office. His work paid off financially: He had a big house, boats, and cars. But his wife became very fed up with him. She left him, ready for divorce.

As a result, He asked Jesus and his wife for forgiveness. They prayed, re- united and left their past lifestyle to serve Christ. They gave away most of their wealth, choosing to live by God's mercy and His guidance.

Then Millard met Clarence, a part time craftsman who guided and taught them about building housing for the poor. They first called it "Partnership Housing."

Millard knew it was his life's calling. When he told people his plans, they said, "Where are you going to get all that money to help the poor with housing?"

He said, ***"We are going to get it from God."***

They said, ***"How?"***

He replied, ***"The fullness of the earth is the Lord's and thereof."*** Habitat for Humanity has helped, built, repaired, or improved over five million homes in many countries worldwide and involved 18 million volunteers and donors.

Does this give you any ideas?

Hugh Jones, former CEO of Barnett Bank in North Florida, said, ***"Habitat for Humanity helped change the culture and productivity of the bank's large processing center. We suffered from so many employees being pressured to get work done that it created bitterness and backbiting. But by appealing to their hearts and asking***

for volunteers, our staff got to know each other as friends and helped needy people on Saturday mornings. Things changed when they were painting and sweating together."

"Our employees became personal friends, staff members were closer, and petty differences disappeared. They became friends and partners. The productivity of their staff improved by 30% by devoting part of Saturdays to help others in need just like God Planned."

Does this apply to your team?

Overcoming the Curse

John D. Rockefeller Sr. (born in 1839 and died in 1937) worked hard to be successful in business. At the age of 33, he became America's first millionaire. At 43, he controlled the biggest company in America, Standard Oil. By 53, he had become the wealthiest man on earth. He was the world's only billionaire at that time (1896).

For his achievement, however, he bartered his happiness and health. He developed Alopecia, a condition in which the hair on his head dropped off (including his eyebrows and eyelashes). One biographer said he looked like a mummy. His weekly income was a million dollars, but his digestion was so bad he could eat only crackers and milk.

Newspapers pictured him as an industrial pirate, and men who worked for him in the oil fields hung him in effigy. Bodyguards watched him day and night. He found little peace or happiness in the wealth that he had accumulated. Rockefeller claimed to be a Christian. At 53, he was frail, and newspapers had already written his obituary.

One night, when he could not sleep, in prayer, he felt God had spoken to him that "his wealth should not hoarded but shared for the benefit of others." The following day, he assembled his staff to establish the Rockefeller Foundation, which has been credited with bettering the lives of humankind since 1913. Much of the money when the time came for it to be distributed as a medicine for Malaria in 1941 came from the Rockefeller Foundation—but the foundation has done more on a broader spectrum.

No one expected him to live past that year. But after that, his health started to improve dramatically. He shocked everyone by not dying until his 98th year. He can still be seen in videos giving money to men, women, and children.

John D. Rockefeller said, ***"The power to make money was a gift from God, just as the instincts for art, music,***

literature, a doctor's talent, and yours—to be developed and used to the best of our ability for the good of mankind. Having been endowed with gifts I possess; I believe it is my duty to make money and still more money and to use the money for the good of my fellowman according to dictates of my conscience."

My opinion: I believe Rockefeller's encounter with God that night before he formed the foundation was the releasing him from the curse or stronghold about to take his life. He lived another 45 years and was giving his wealth away. They continue to give it away today.

Does this apply to you?

People may want to criticize and curse the Rockefeller Foundation today for the liberal activities they have supported for decades. That does not diminish this story of how God can extend a man's life and calling. Did God allow John D. to gain wealth to hoard it? No. All of us should be praying for the Rockefeller family and staff to invest in what serves God's greatest purposes. Will you join me?

Overcoming the Stronghold of Fear

When I was hosting a daily radio show called Inspiration316, I searched for more testimonies and stories of Christ working in people's lives. Through the Christian Healing Ministry formed by **Francis and Judith McNutt**, I met a woman who told me how God had healed her heart in the middle of one of the Christian healing ministry classes.

Her story started when she was just eight years old, and her mom and dad decided to divorce. As her dad was walking out of the front door, she remembered crying, pulling on his arm, and screaming, ***"Daddy, don't leave,"*** and kept repeating, ***"Daddy, don't leave."***

It did not stop him; she vividly remembered him packing his car and never looking back. At that moment, evil thoughts came all over her. She had been abandoned.

She was so excited when she told me her story with a giant smile. She could not wait to tell me how God spoke to her that day, healing her aching heart after so many years. She had never learned ***"God can speak to you"*** in her church. She had worried for 15 years that her husband and kids would abandon her, that any day she was going to lose her job. In that workshop, on that day, she heard the Lord say, ***"You are healed. You will not be abandoned. I will always be with you. Trust in me all your days and I will never leave you."***

Hallelujah!!

Should you seek Wise Counsel?

Unforgiveness, but why?

Kathi Smith tells the story of her youngest son, who, at three years old, continued to throw up every morning no matter where he was. It could have been in the kitchen, at the supermarket, or outside playing. She never knew where and when. One day at a neighbor's house, he threw up, and the neighbor said, "***Take that kid to the Christian Healing Ministry. They will pray for him, and God can heal him.***"

She replied, ***"My PASTOR never teaches us how to pray for healing."***

The neighbor persisted. ***"Just do it."***

So, finally, she did. Her son played on the floor as leaders prayed for him. No one touched him. The next day, he said to his mom, ***"I did not throw up today, and you did not even give me my medicine."***

Kathi said, ***"Wonderful."*** He never had a problem again.But within six months, she was in a wheelchair, feeling trapped. She could not use one of her legs. She was in a great deal of pain and was unable to prepare meals for her family. The doctor said, "Take these drugs. You will need them for the rest of your life."

She said, "No thanks; I am going to Christian Healing Ministry." After one session with a team of two intercessors praying, she felt some relief. But when it was still hurting, she scheduled another prayer session. The night before, she cried out to God and begged Him to heal her. She heard the Lord say in her spirit, ***"There will be someone there who will explain your needs."***

As she sat with the intercessors, she asked, ***"Did either of you hear from the Lord about my healing?"***

They both looked at each other and said, ***"No."***

However, an intern in the room was observing and learning how to pray for others. She said, ***"I believe there was something about a kidnapping. Did that happen to you?"***

Kathi replied, ***"Yes. When I was a young girl, we lived in Lebanon. My parents worked in the U.S. Foreign Service there. One afternoon, another friend and I were studying alone in our apartment. A man broke in and kidnapped us. He threw us in the back of his car. He was looking for ransom. As he rapidly drove out of the city,***

traffic was crazy, stop and go. When he stopped the sixth time and could not move we jumped out of the car and ran home safely. This was before 'seat belts'."

The intern said, ***"The Lord told me something about forgiveness."***

Kathi said, ***"Forgiveness?"*** Pondering, finally she said, ***"OK, Lord, I forgive the man who did that to us."*** The intercessors then prayed over her leg. She got out of the wheelchair and walked. And she never had a leg problem again. Kathi and her husband have greatly supported the Christian Healing Ministry ever since.

Does this give you ideas?

Examples of common strongholds
or deep hurt the enemy uses.

- ✓ "Sticks and stones may hurt you, but name-calling will never hurt you." - That's a lie that never leaves until Christ removes them.
- ✓ Name-calling or any sexual or physical abuse in your ancestry that gives Satan the right to torment

and control strongholds in your life for five generations.

- ✓ Very little or no love from parents,
- ✓ Raised in Foster care without love.
- ✓ Yelling or fighting with parents or relatives
- ✓ People/kids calling you names.
- ✓ Teacher embarrassing you in class
- ✓ Sexual molestation as a kid or adult
- ✓ Natural feeling of insecurity as a child that never leaves
- ✓ Satan places guilt or shame on you through the voices or thoughts you receive.

-18-

How to Praise Yourself to Better Health.

— Proverbs 17:22 —

"A joyful heart is good medicine, but a crushed spirit dries the bones,"

— Ecclesiastes 9:7-9 —

'Cheerfulness of the spirit has a great influence upon the body and contributes to the health and welfare of it."

'Go, eat your food with gladness, and drink your wine with a joyful heart, for God has already approved what you do…'

Praise raises the spirit, invigorates the body, and prepares it for service and business.

Overcoming Cancer

Jordan Rubin's journey is a testament to the power of faith, a positive mindset, and healthy living in overcoming health challenges. As a cheerleader at Florida State University, he was diagnosed with Crohn's disease, a condition that can severely affect the intestinal tract. Despite the devastating impact of the disease, Jordan's determination to find a holistic solution led him to explore options, including surgery, drugs, and diets.

One day, a doctor told him the answer was in the Bible —about food a person should eat. It took a long time trusting that God would lead him with the right foods as described in the Bible and prayers. It did happen, and an outgrowth was the founding of **Garden of Life**, one of America's top Health Food companies. This story of faith and perseverance is a beacon of hope for those facing health challenges.

However, about eight years later, he discovered he had kidney cancer, and doctors said he would die within a year if he did not have surgery, plus Chemotherapy. He had even authored a book on healing cancer. He cried out to God, ***"What do I do?"*** Within two weeks, his cancer number went from 220 to 280, and he was devastated. Doctors gave him little chance to live.

He still cried out to God with his face on the floor. He challenged God to heal him and tested God's faithfulness over many months to remove the cancer through three benchmarks. Each of these were in the midst of joy and fear. But God won. His cancer score went to zero.

Jordan reminds us of Romans 12:2: *"Do not conform to the pattern of this world but be transformed by the renewing of your mind. Then you can test and accept God's will—his good, pleasing, and perfect will."*

Cancer Centers of America has eight centers in the USA, and the chaplain interviews each patient and 61% of the Cancer patients agree to having unforgiveness issues. Doctors say unforgiveness breaks down your immune system and made you more vulnerable to cancer.

Can that be one of the causes of cancer,

or does it hinder its healing?

Does this give your ideas?

Unforgiveness is one of Satan's favorite tools.

I had the opportunity to study and read about Apple's tremendous success and impact. I have used a Mac from my earliest days with a computer and studied **Steve Jobs's** life.

It is not a well-known fact that Steve was the result of an affair. His mom gave him up for adoption to the Jobs family, who promised to send him to college. His father was from the Middle East and eventually owned a restaurant in the Bay area.

The insecurity thoughts of ***"you weren't wanted"*** left him with feelings of being abandoned and drove him to succeed in the world. He was always trying to prove himself and tough out every obstacle. He was visionary, driven to find solutions, bold, and arrogant. He and **Steve Wozniak** made great breakthroughs with their minicomputer. They changed the industry and rocked the arrogant IBM and Microsoft companies.

In my opinion, what killed Steve was this: Satan will torment you with thoughts of you were "unwanted." If Steve had come to know Christ and asked for forgiveness for his own sins, the Lord would have convicted him to go to his father to forgive him. He spoke to his mother but never forgave his father. He knew where his Father was but never reached out to him.

I have firsthand experience of someone very close to me

who died of pancreatic cancer. This revelation underscores the importance of forgiveness in maintaining good health and empowers us to let go of grudges. I referenced the **Cancer Centers of America** survey earlier.

Many factors: a poor diet or nutrition, lack of prayer, counseling, and harmful medical treatments can lead to dying too young. Christ died on the cross for our sins; The Lord God sent Jesus to take the rap for us. Steve chose Hinduism as his faith. Is it possible that if he had believed or reached out to Jesus Christ, he might have lived to an old age, like John D. Rockefeller and JC Penney?

Does this apply to you?

Years ago, I discovered some physical challenges, especially digestive issues, which led me to a desire to be healthier.

- ✓ I discovered there is more calcium in broccoli than milk (vs. what milk advertising had led me to believe in my younger years).
- ✓ I discovered through trips to Europe how they ate differently and were healthier than Americans.
- ✓ I changed my diet and started taking many vitamins

I learned about from an Austrian woman. She uses a hand cradle system and Bioenergetic system that stimulates my circulatory system.

- ✓ What does this mean? I test via a bioenergetic system, which has been used in Germany for many years. The body has its own electrical and energy system that flows from your toes to the tops of your head. It's like an X-ray system, noting your essential organs' strengths and weaknesses.
- ✓ I discovered colon cleanses. I believed I had inherited issues with my colon from my mom, who had a foot and a half of her colon removed; I did colon cleanses (again more prominent in Europe), which made a big difference for me. I eat more fiber and drink more water (including Mineral water), which most Europeans do.
- ✓ I discovered that our body also has an electrical system with impulses from light and sound that heal our body internally, even moving our blood 30% faster, as discovered in German systems.
- ✓ I bought an Infrared Sauna for our home that I have used now for 25 years. Since I don't sweat easily, it has been refreshing, cleansing, removing toxins, etc. This is a key reason I believe why my metabolic age is just 54, but my chronological age is 83; I bought and used more exercise equipment for my home.

Does this apply to you?

Revelation

I don't like exercising and find it boring, but I want and need it. While praying one night, the Lord told me, ***"Pull out your cell phone and start listening to praise music while you exercise."***

The rest is history. Boredom left me, and exercise became enjoyable as I prayed to Him through the Word found in his song and the Holy Spirit, who led songwriters to create the lyrics. Satan does not like how I smell because I have on the Aroma of God.

Result

✓ Today, Exercising is not dull but FUN.

✓ I use a Whole-Body Vibrator for 10 minutes daily to increase blood flow and strengthen my legs and balance. Just 10 min equals a mile of jogging, but you are just standing.

✓ The Sound waves that heal throughout your body, through your muscles, breathing, bones, and blood flow.

- ✓ Another aspect of my personal exercise plan - I can't stand still when a good song moves me. I want to clap my hands or swing back and forth, moving with the beat of the music. I feel harmony with the music or singing, especially with a praise song. Good praise music repeats the Word of God, which is scripture. Remember what I said? ***"The word of God which is sharper than a double-edged sword."*** You are creating the Aroma or Incense of God that the enemy hates. He does not want to be near you.

Does this apply to you?

-19-

Praise is a Weapon -

Phil Driscoll is one of the best concert trumpet players ever. He has played the trumpet for 60 years, studied as a musician, pilot, and evangelist.

Here is some of his wisdom.

"The loving sound is Food from Heaven."

God is the Spirit. Praising scripture by song is Spiritual Food. Praise is the rocket full of Victory. A football team needs a crowd's praise to reach its highest level of performance.

Praise puts a force field around your life if you do it from your heart each day. If you praise Him even during tough times, you will be protected. You have heard… "God inhabits the Praises of His People."

Too many Christians are flying with too little thrust. The deeper the praise of God, the stronger your thrust is to fly above the storms in your life.

You were born to rise about your challenge.

- ✓ Praise is rocket fuel for your triumph. You can't praise and be in the battle at the same time.
- ✓ Praise it like the thrust in an airplane.
- ✓ God does business in the law of fair exchange, sowing, and reaping.

The closest thing to God's heart is a worshiper.

Satan does not like a worshiper. The more you praise God in worship, the more energy you will reap from Him, including His healing power and fruitfulness. God is releasing his energy through the sounds of praise to Him.

- ✓ We will spend most of our time praising Him in Heaven. It should be "done on earth as if it is in heaven."
- ✓ Praise music is the anthem of God.

Join me in finding the healing power of God within God's plans for you."

Phil's wife, Darlene, is a Pastor, says, ***"Tell my people the WORD says, 'My Words are Voice Activated.'"***

Believe in God's Word and positive claims and beliefs. Claim the Word over yourself and others. I repeat: ***"Faith***

comes by hearing His word." Verbal expression speeds mental acceptance. Once the brain keeps hearing you repeating and claiming His words and positive thoughts, it starts to reprogram your thinking from the world's ways to God's ways over Satan's stinking thinking.

Does this apply to you?

Revelation

God knew the Treasure He buried in your heart. Again, the sound of His words, containers of emotions, His Spirit of love, and so much more connected me with Him.

— 1 John 2:27 —

"But as his anointing teaches you about all things, and all that is anointing is But as his anointing is real, not counterfeit, remain in him."

The anointing is the Holy Spirit living within those who have believed in Jesus as Lord. This anointing refers to the Holy Spirit's ability to help believers understand what is right and wrong.

"Praise His Name" Song Anyway

by Jeff & Sheri Easter

When you're up against a wall and
your mountain seems so tall

And you realize that life's not always fair

You can run away and hide, let the old man decide

Or you can change your circumstances with a prayer

When everything falls apart praise His name

When you have a broken heart
raise your hands and say

Lord, You're all I need, You're everything to me

And He'll take the pain away

When it seem you're all alone praise His name

When you feel you can't go on
just raise your hands and say

Greater is He that is within me

And you can praise the hurt away
if you'll just praise His name

Oh, you can overcome by the blood of the lamb

And by the word of your testimony

You'll see the darkness go as your faith begins to grow

You're not alone so how can you be lonely

When everything falls apart praise His name

When you have a broken heart
raise your hands and say

Lord, You're all I need, You're everything to me

And He'll take the pain away

When it seem you're all alone praise His name

When you feel you can't go on
just raise your hands and say

Greater is He that is within me

And you can praise the hurt away
(And you can praise the hurt away)

Greater is He that is within me

You can praise the hurt away
if you'll just praise His name

Written by: Jerry Bruce Haynes, Lee Hendrix
Album: Miles and Milestones
Released: 2005
Lyrics provided by Musixmatch

-20-

What is Science Telling Us

Where Faith meets physics, healing through strategies in quantum mechanics.

Dr. Caroline Leaf:

The Brain, Mind, Body Connection

Dr. Caroline Leaf is a communication pathologist and cognitive neuroscientist. Since the early '80s, she has researched the mind-brain connection, the nature of mental health, and the formation of memory. She was one of the first in her field to study how the brain can change, also known as neuroplasticity, with dedicated mind input.

Here are excerpts of a podcast interview with her.

Moderator Abel: For the geeks like me out there, neuroplasticity is a fascinating thing. So why don't we start right there? What is neuroplasticity for people unfamiliar with it, and why is it so encouraging?

Carolyn: ***"Well, it's encouraging, Abel, because it shows that, yes, the brain can change. Back in the '80s, when I was doing my initial research, we were trained that our brain couldn't change, that once our brain's fixed, that's it. You've got to deal with it."***

At that time, I thought, *'Just by how we think and our state of mind. No, this is false because we instinctively know that we influence ourselves.'*

"And working with patients with traumatic brain injuries and various neurological issues, I saw that the ones who were more determined and deliberate about their work would change. So, I started a series of research studies, and they showed that, as you use your mind deliberately, you can change behavioral function, cognition, intelligence, social-emotional function, and just about everything else about how you function."

"We had C.T. scans then, but MRI was only developed in the mid-'90s. It has shown us how the brain can respond to the mind. So, from that brain technology, we started getting insight into the fact that, as you think, you change the structure of your brain. That's so powerful. Neuroplasticity is the ability of our minds to change our brains. This means that the mind is separate from the brain, but the mind works through the brain, and the brain responds to the mind. And neuroplasticity is how we use our mind to change the structure of our brain in different directions. And it keeps changing."

"The brain can't change itself. The brain is changed by what you're thinking, feeling, choosing, and what you're eating. There is scientific proof that Sound Wave frequencies bring physical, mental, and spiritual healing to your body."

I have experienced some of the new equipment (vibragenix) founded by **Dr. Caroline Stites**, which is effective and brings physical healing. It even combines with RIFE technology discovered years ago in Europe. She says, ***"Our body is 70% water, and sound travels faster through water."***

The Proof is that ***sound frequencies heal the body,*** primarily through the Word of God received in your spirit and repeated repeatedly.

KEY: It keeps evil and demons away from us. It is the aroma and incense of God. Evil can't stand to be in the presence of God. Remember, the skunk protects himself. It is like our Mosquito "Satan" repellent, which the Lord planned to protect us.

Does this apply to you?

From a Neuroscientist's perspective

Dr. Darlene Lobel is a neurosurgeon, neuroscientist, and the author of ***The Science of God's Healing Power and How to Walk on Fire.*** She is based in Florida and still performs brain surgery, but she takes time to operate her ministry, ***"Healing in the Kingdom,"*** with over 200 disciples and coaches. She explains how the brain functions with sounds, music, exercise, etc.

She explains that ***"when listening to or participating in appealing and loving music, dopamine is released. It's a hormone that causes your body to feel good, especially in your brain cells. It elevates your mood and instantly makes you feel happier."***

Is it a natural medicine the body makes?

Does this apply to you?

When active individuals venture beyond their comfort zone, they often experience a profound sense of joy and liberation. This shift in environment can elevate your mood, especially when accompanied by a playlist of your favorite tunes, which triggers the release of dopamine. In addition to physical exercise, activities like dancing also stimulate the production of dopamine in your body, further enhancing your happiness.

The brain is active among a group of cells known as mirror neurons, which start to cause you to move almost like a dancing gesture, moving your arms and your head with the beat just like your heartbeat, but at a faster pace—some of the same things you want to do, especially when dancing.

In times of prayer, even holding hands with others as you pray is a great moment for social bonding. It reduces fear, and you're more likely to be adventurous and step out of your comfort zone in this state. You open yourself up to trust others around you more.

Next, you'll learn and develop more lasting relationships— all related to brain activity, hormones, and stimuli. Hugging can significantly boost oxytocin, again elevating the mood even more. A sense of bonding, oxytocin even reduces fear and makes you feel like you can accomplish anything.

All of this stimulates your imagination, and the vision God can give a person. It's a basis of hopes, dreams, and visions of things you hope to accomplish that God gives you. This is where your mirror neurons come into play as you visualize stuff around you, including things you've never touched

As different parts of your brain become more active, the faster you see your image come to fruition, connecting between neurons in the brain. Again, more activity to see new observations and change your perspective. This causes new pathways to be formed in your brain and the new groove, creating that fire together. They are wired together, and you see yourself going to be on what you might not normally expect.

Can combat release that same dopamine?

— John 10:27 —

"My sheep listen to my voice;
I know them, and they follow me."

Does this apply to you?

-21-

This is the Lord Speaking.

D**ick Erickson**, a young man raised on a Farm in North Dakota, was no stranger to hard work. His parents, devout in their faith, took him to church and prayed for him constantly. Little did he know their prayers would lead him on a journey of faith and transformation.

There were too many temptations in his first year in college, so he flunked out. When Uncle Sam called, he went to Vietnam as a marine. He learned to be a helicopter pilot and, within a year had done hundreds of reconnaissance flights picking up marines who needed to be rescued from Vietcong battles.

One night, their commanding officer ordered them to pick up a captured Viet Cong leader for interrogation and bring him back to base. They got to their destination in the middle of the night. They picked up the captured Vietcong and started back to base during unfriendly fire.

They only heard static as they radioed for guidance to get back to base. ***"Base come in, base come in, base come in,"*** they repeated. They could not reach the base, which was dangerous because they had little visibility to see trees, roads, mountains, etc. Finally, they heard a voice: ***"This is the Lord, and I will guide you back to base."*** In shock, they heard little but followed as the Spirit guided them.

As they landed safely, the three pilots looked at each other and asked if they heard a voice. They all said YES. Do you think that was the Lord? They prayed and thanked the Lord. Dick still tells the story today.

He committed to living for Christ and built a $20 million and successful tire business. He built his company on Biblical principles and has been a strong witness as he has served Christ. Dick authored his story in his book, ***How the Rubber Meets the Road***. He often sites

— Psalm 23 —

THE LORD is my shepherd, I lack nothing.

2 *He makes me lie down in green pastures, he leads me beside quiet waters,*

3 *he refreshes my soul. He guides me along the right paths for his name's sake.*

4 Even though I walk through the darkest valley,[a] I will fear no evil, for you are with me; your rod and your staff, they comfort me.

5 You prepare a table before me in the presence of my enemies. You anoint my head with oil; my cup overflows.

6 Surely your goodness and love will follow me all the days of my life, and I will dwell in the house of the LORD forever.

Every day, take a few minutes to visualize yourself in God's passion for you to achieve new heights and abide with him. Then, cortisol is heightened, which reduces stress. Finally, serotonin is released during singing, making you more aware of memory, neurological processes, numerous psychological processes, and a sense of reward. Recognition and learning are stimulated by singing and praising the Father, who created us.

Worship is not just a ritual. It is a vital aspect of a believer's relationship with God. It is a way to express our love, adoration, and gratitude toward Him. As John 4:23 says, 'But the hour is coming, and is now here, when the true worshippers will worship the Father in spirit and truth for the Father is seeking such people to worship him.' God seeks those who will worship Him with sincerity and authenticity, strengthening the bond between the believer and the divine.

—John 4:23—

God seeks those who will worship Him
with sincerity and authenticity.

Should you seek Wise Counsel?

-22-

Can God Use a Crash to Save Thousands?

Can you imagine one afternoon after you had dropped your wife and two boys at the airport and learned from your father there was a plane crash near Denver? You then realize that is the same connecting flight you put your family on. That is precisely what happened to **Tony Nasrallah** and his family. Tony immediately prayed, calling airlines, city officials, police, and hospitals, but there were no answers. Finally, he discovered that 28 people had died, but 53 walked off the plane safely.

He was sure the Lord had protected his family from harm. Tony and his mother flew to Denver, believing his wife and children would be okay. Upon arrival in Denver, he learned that his children were not on the survivors list. He also discovered that medical personnel had transported nine people who were in critical care units to local hospitals.

One woman, who they thought was a 50-year-old, could not be identified. His wife, Anne, was twenty-two. ***"Could this be his wife?"*** At first, he said, "I don't know?" He saw a woman with a shaved head three times its normal size. The woman was in a coma.

The doctor said, ***"We are trying to keep her alive. She is connected to survival devices. She has lost so much blood, and she may not live through the night."***

Finally, Tony looked at the woman's wedding band. It was Anne. He was allowed to see the bodies of his boys through a big glass window, but they would not let him touch or pray for them. Tony said, ***"It was tormenting."*** He kept thinking, ***"God, why did you let this happen? Was I not deserving enough? Have I not been a loyal believer? Yes! It was Anne!! but she is barely alive!"*** He called home and asked friends to pray!!!

After sleepless nights in her room with her, Tony started to get sick himself. They said he had PTSD. They wanted to admit him. He refused to leave Anne. Each day, she got a little better, and for weeks, he slept by her side and kept praying over her. But the voice in his head kept saying, ***"When she dies, take that big chair and smash the hospital window and jump out the 28th floor and commit suicide to join your family in heaven...you fool."***

Close friends called and prayed. Three friends even

traveled to Denver to see them and pray for Anne. Tony and Anne were in Denver for three months before they could return to their Jacksonville home. Anne was in rehab for many years, improving. Then, unexpectedly, they had two more boys.

In gratefulness, Tony asked the Lord, ***"How can I not obey the plan for me to serve my God?"*** He was open to serving the Lord and had a vision. He wanted to replicate an old coffee house that featured Christian bands and music that had encouraged his early walk with Christ. So, for three years, he sought a venue where he could do that.

Doubters told Tony, ***"You cannot do that without alcohol; you will lose your shirt."*** Then, when Tony found an abandoned old movie theatre, he felt the Lord's blessing and vision and stepped out in faith to create the Murry Hill Theatre.

For 30 years, the Murray Hill Theatre has hosted hundreds of music groups and entertainment for 350,000 believers and nonbelievers without alcoholic beverages, to Satan's great disappointment. Thousands have come to Christ, met their spouses, volunteered to serve, and sparked the revival of a beaten-down neighborhood. Today, Anne has no brain damage and is a master viola player. She is a member of a Christian Witness Orchestra, and she and Tony travel throughout the world to serve the Lord.

"God has a Plan to strengthen us
to accomplish His plan."

Does this apply to you?

-23-

Christian Religion vs Relationship

Backgound

In 1980, I had an evil encounter that rocked me and caused me to seek the Lord in deep and submissive prayer—asking Him to take over and lead me for the rest of my life.

Within just a few weeks, the Lord led me to the business I had run for 14 years, which became an absolute blessing to me and CEOs throughout Florida.

During that time, I had been attending a mainline denomination church with my family. The joy I experienced in my new spirit led life to come alive for Christ. I received an absolute passion and heart to help the church relate to people more deeply and gain their compassion to serve. I shared my testimony with a

Monsignor, and he was excited to hear it. He wanted me to share it with others and meet the Bishop. So he set up an appointment for us to come together, the three of us, in the Bishop's office. The Monsignor explained a little bit about my background and then asked me to tell the Bishop my desire to serve. I told the Bishop I was a Born Again Christian, born of the spirit, and had a passion and hunger to help the church grow and improve, reach more people, etc. After sharing my conviction, the Bishop said something that rocked my world. He said, "Don't worry about it. You'll get over that."

Yet, I recalled many years earlier visiting the Vatican and discovered that Peter was buried there as the church's first Pope and Christ said, ***"Upon this Rock, Peter, I will build my church."*** I Peter 1:22-23 says, ***"Now that you have purified yourselves by the Truth so that you have sincere love for your brothers. Love one another deeply from the heart, for you have been 'Born Again' not a perishable seed but imperishable seed through living and enduring the word of God."*** Imperishable means the true heart is of the Spirit never to perish, always alive in your heart.

The Bible refers to Born of the Spirit of God. God is Spirit. He created this spirit within us, the Spirit does not come alive until we ask for His forgiveness and submit to Him in walking and led by Christ through the Holy Spirit.

Replying to Nicodemus, the Jewish Pharisee, Jesus

said in John 3:7: *"Jesus said, I tell you the truth, no man can see the Kingdom of God unless he is born again?"* to which Nicodemus replied, ***"how can a man be born again out of a mother's womb, and Jesus replied I tell you the truth no man can enter the kingdom of God unless he is born of water and the spirit, his birth to flesh, but the spirit gives birth to spirit you should not be surprised at me that you must be born again. It's like the wind blows wherever it pleases you hear it sound, but you cannot tell it comes from where it's going, so it is whatever Born of the spirit."***

Then, in verse 12, He says, ***"I have spoken to you of earthly things, and you do not believe, how then will you believe? If I speak of heavenly things "words, you don't understand them, he continues. The Son of man must be lifted up that everyone who believes in Him has eternal life… work for God loves the world that he gave his one and only begotten Son that whoever believes in Him, he will not perish but have eternal life. For God did not send his Son into the world to condemn the world to save the world through Him (break the power of evil and gives Grace), whoever believes in Him is not condemned."***

And later he says in verse 20, ***Everyone who does evil hates the light, and will not come into the light for fear that their deeds will be exposed. 21 But whoever lives by the truth comes into the light, so that it may be seen***

plainly that what they have done has been done in the sight of God."

Looking through My Father's Eyes

Are churches following the Christian Religious principles or a true Relationship with Jesus Christ?

Have many of today's churches dropped the command to be "Born of the Spirit" and called "Born Again" as Jesus and Peter described? Remember we are first Spirit, as is God himself.

Are Pastors afraid of convicting people to seek the Lord and to be obedient to their individual calling? Are Pastors fearful of what people might say about them? So, are Pastors or Priests just offering Sunday services that use scripture highlights with no convictions? Programing for the masses? Are they simply following what the Seminary told them and not seeking for themselves? Do some Pastors of mainline denominations confess Jesus but not seek His leading? What is the relationship God wants most from us? Religion or Relationship ?

Many members of these mainline denominations are religious and believe that Christ died for our sins, which is all good, but do not seek Him to guide their lives. Yet many of these churches still offer communion and baptism but no longer confession or asking for forgiveness.

Seeing through my Fathers Eyes

I believe Christ wants most is our personal relationship with Him while knowing and studying the Word, praying, praising and following His leading. We need Christian Religion but Christ is seeking more...A Relationship that is personal, friendship and submissive. Pursuing our calling. Most Chrisitians don't know their calling.

They are living in tradition…Christian Religion.

The three tools that make Christianity work in a Personal Relationship with Christ are:

1. Studying the word and seeking to hear His voice for guidance answering your prayers is critical in Christianity
2. Prayer and Praise songs. or through praise
3. Fully loving relationship with Christ personally

Many good people have been morally good and care for one another, but the same people and do nothing about resisting evil. They often miss the joy of knowing Christ to be guided by Him to fulfill his deepest purposes in their lives.

The best contributions of these churches are the volunteer, family relationships, schools, and community service they create or administer. We need them, but we are living in a time when the Lord is calling us to hear His voice, His calling personally, and to be obedient to His will. Some of the main churches are splitting or being modified by "Woke" groups with different sexual orientations. I am not an expert on any of this, but the question has the mainline churches lost focus on being “Born Again” and hearing from the Holy Spirit for “tradition”? One Pastor told a business associate of mine he is going with changes in his demonization because he is more concerned about his retirement than his teaching or leading his flock for the deeper things of Christ.

What makes the core of Christianity stronger than other Religions is a Personal Relationship with God though Jesus.

In this book I share many life changing experiences through brokenness and submission to Christ in personal and even business callings. This relationship is personal, hearing and recognizing when the Lord is leading you, and answering your prayers. I have met with a Muslim and my best understanding is that Mohammad created Islam. That both Mohammed and Jesus and he are prophets God is Aliah, Jesus never died on the cross. Most Muslims attend Mosque once a week. They’re supposed to worship and pray five times a day on their knees. It’s about a religion. Not a relationship.

In the Koran, Jesus (known as Isa in Arabic) is mentioned 25 times by name. Additionally, he is referred to by various titles and descriptions, which collectively account for a total of 78 mentions of Jesus when including these titles. I have heard testimonies from several, who say there is no personal relationship with God. Christianity is about a beloved God to worship, a relationship with Christ the son of God and His leading.

Is praise music and even many hymns the best Personal Relationship Tool for the Lord? Is the music heart felt? Music requires your voice and a sincere heart to sing and grow in relationship with Him.

Can it or does praise replace or improve personal church worship?

Derek Prince, author of ***"Blessings and Curses, you Choose"*** Sincere Praise imposes silence on the enemy. His book is a very powerful tool to be protected from Spiritual attacks. He was quoted in the 1990s as saying that "God was going to create a generation of people who would praise his name. He believes the charismatic movement has been the beginning of that especially among younger people."

Derek continued, ***"God has been saying through the ages, "I have been waiting for a generation to praise me as I have wanted."*** He quotes Jesus in Matthew 21 saying that ***"my God is perfecting a people of praise."***

Derrick Prince was born in India, but raised in Great Britain, traveled to 20 different countries, and wrote 60 books. Derick says, ***"Praise is such a key and God was sending a new generation of believers who were going to praise God and sing and in a movement."*** He believes it sparked the charismatic movement as it is today. This demonstrated what God had shown him to happen back in the 1980s.

-24-

Cancer - a Blessing or a Curse?

J**im Francis** an Attorney, and former CEO of Charter Oil a billion dollar company, got cancer in his thyroid and Doctors immediately removed it from him. He felt in good hands of one the top clinics in America. But their concern became very large when they said he had a 5% chance of living the next five years. Jim, a man of great Faith and Bible teacher in his own home did not have fear of dying. Yet his family was very shaken and friends around him as well. But his wife had received a book from a friend of the Christian Healing ministry that was entitled ***"Blessings and Curses You Choose"*** by former Pastor and worldwide teacher **Derick Prince**. Derek had spoken in 20 countries and wrote 60 books and still has many teachings on YouTube even though he passed away in the 1990s.

Physicians were very concerned and tested Jim many times over five years, even though Jim claimed he'd been healed through an encounter with Christ and the Holy Spirit. Plus he received individual prayer time at the Christian Healing Ministry who confirmed his healing. Yet, skeptical Physicians continued to test Jim with his consent and insurance companies. ***Finally, they confessed it was a miracle.***

Jim said the book gave him a new perspective on life and that we are all going to die yet live forever, if we submitted our lives in service to Christ.

Jim had a spiritual encounter with the Lord and felt a healing in his body and spirit as he read the book. His wife afraid to read the book finally did and broke down and cried for four days realizing the revelation and the insight that it provided for her, her family and husband.

Cancer Centers of America has eight centers in the USA, and the chaplain interviews each patient and 61% of the Cancer patients agree to having unforgiveness issues.

Doctors say unforgiveness breaks down your immunesystem and makes you more vulnerable to cancer.

Back Pain
or a way to take me deeper ?

Years ago, after selling my previous business, I used to get up every morning, do 20 push-ups, and stretch my legs to touch my toes. It was a good habit and helped me be stronger and more flexible. But one morning, when I got up, I was in such a state that I couldn't even do either one push-up or stretching. That went on for at least six months, and during that time, I went to MDs, Chiropractors, and Acupuncture professionals without any real satisfaction or relief. At the same time, I was attending a new church where the Pastor each Sunday would say from the beginning of each service. ***"Who needs a healing in here?"***

By faith, I would stand up, with typically only 12 different people each Sunday out of at least 1000 in attendance. My pride was embarrassed. He didn't individually pray for us, but he did say a general prayer for all of us.

As I was shaving, looking into the mirror, I spoke to the Lord and said, ***"Lord, how come you never healed me of that back pain?"***

And the Lord spoke to me profoundly in my thoughts and said, ***"Because you'll give all that credit to the vitamin you take."*** Immediately, I realized He was right, even though he was the one that led me to take vitamins from a woman from Europe using a sophisticated system of analysis for different health issues.

Then I realized, ***"God is a jealous God. He wants credit for a healing."*** He wants credit for the things He's done for us to witness to other people, so I knew He was right. He deserves credit. So, I kept praying and asking God for healing. Within two months, the pain was gone entirely.

This taught me another lesson about trusting Him and witnessing Him. I should not give credit to the world when the solution was in the Lord. It was not the vitamins, or big Pharma.

God had the solution.

Severe Tooth Pain or Learning How to trust

I had a very severe tooth pain on the right upper side of my mouth that was driving me crazy. All the things I tried to do naturally did not seem to stop the pain. In talking to my health advisor, she recommended an exceptional dentist in Orlando who treated things more naturally rather than just trying to stick in another filling, put a cap on it, root canal, or pull it.

Seeing the new dentist seemed like a practical idea, so I set up an appointment with him, but then he canceled the appointment because he had to go out of town for Thanksgiving. So, I had to wait another month before I could get in to see him.

One night, the pain was so severe I was lying in a fetal position in my bed crying out to God for healing. I prayed without ceasing for four hours. Finally, the Lord reminded me of a Bible story.

I cried, " ***Lord, I will tell 7,000 people if you heal this tooth."*** Within less than 30 minutes, all the pain went away.

I still did not see the dentist for another 30 days. He told me, ***"That tooth is completely broken in half; there is no way you could live without severe pain. It's a Miracle."***

-25-

The Untold Secret to Finding Peace and Harmony Within Yourself.

"Jesus asked "how you should pray, says...'Our Father in heaven, hallowed be your name, 10 your kingdom come, your will be done,on earth as it is in heaven....so we know that people and angels PRAISE God in heaven— Should we do the same on earth?

—Matthew 6:10—

Take on His Aroma

"God Inhabits the Praises of His people."

—Colossians 3:16 NIV—

16 Let the message of Christ dwell among you richly as you teach and admonish one another with all wisdom through psalms, hymns, and songs from the Spirit, singing to God with gratitude in your hearts.

—Ephesians 5:1—

Follow God's example, therefore, as dearly loved children 2 and walk in the way of love, just as Christ loved us and gave himself up for us as a fragrant offering and sacrifice to God.

18 Do not get drunk on wine, which leads to debauchery. Instead, be filled with the Spirit, 19 speaking to one another with psalms, hymns, and songs from the Spirit. Sing and make music from your heart to the Lord, 20 always giving thanks to God the Father for everything, in the name of our Lord Jesus Christ.

Look through these scriptures.

Does they tell you something?

Do they confirm what I am saying?

"Praise God all day and night, and you will stink to Satan and take on the aroma of God and the shield of protection which envelopes with and the love, joy and peace of your Creator."

Confirming scriptures following are about praise songs and hymns:

(Not all songs are entirely from repeated scripture, but the majority comes through the leading of the Holy Spirit, just like scripture penned by the Old Testament elders and disciples and today by songwriters seeking the Lord as they write.)

Psalms 92,

a song fools do not understand,

1 It is good to praise the Lord and
make music to your name, O Most High,

2 proclaiming your love in the morning
and your faithfulness at night,

3 to the music of the ten-stringed lyre
and the melody of the harp.

4 For you make me glad by your deeds, Lord;
I sing for joy at what your hands have done.

5 How great are your works,
Lord, how profound your thoughts!

6 Senseless people do not know,
fools do not understand

7 that though the wicked spring up like grass and all
evildoers flourish, they will be destroyed forever.

8 But you, Lord, are forever exalted.

9 For surely your enemies, Lord, surely your enemies will
perish; all evildoers will be scattered.

10 You have exalted my horn[b] like that of a wild ox;
fine oils have been poured on me.

11 My eyes have seen the defeat of my adversaries; my
ears have heard the rout of my wicked foes.

12 The righteous will flourish like a palm tree, they will
grow like a cedar of Lebanon;

13 planted in the house of the Lord,
they will flourish in the courts of our God.

14 They will still bear fruit in old age,
they will stay fresh and green,

15 proclaiming, "The Lord is upright;
he is my Rock, and there is no wickedness in him."

Psalm 30:4

4 Sing the praises of the Lord, you his faithful people;
praise his holy name.

Psalm 147:1 Praise the Lord. [a]

How good it is to sing praises to our God,
how pleasant and fitting to praise him!

Psalm 66:8

8 Praise our God, all peoples,

let the sound of his praise be heard;

Psalm 67:3

3 May the peoples praise you, God;

may all the peoples praise you.

Romans 15:9

Therefore, I will praise you among the Gentiles;

I will sing the praises of your name." [a]

1 Peter 2:9

9 But you are a chosen people, a royal priesthood,
a holy nation, God's special possession,
that you may declare the praises of him
who called you out of darkness into his wonderful light.

Luke 1:68

"Praise be to the Lord, the God of Israel, because he has come to his people and redeemed them."

What is the number one thing they do in Heaven??

.... They praise God.

As Jesus said in Matthew 6:10, *"Your kingdom come, Your will be done, on earth as it is in Heaven."*

Or Matthew 18:19: *"Again, truly I tell you that if two of you on earth agree about anything they ask for, it will be done for them by my Father in heaven."*

Inspiring Songs from the Word

These are just some of my favorite songs that can alter your thinking and put you in harmony with your Creator and Lord Jesus Christ.

These songs are only examples of songs, praises, and hymns that use or convey the word of God around and in you. It's your Aroma again, Your Armor and Praise weapon.

1. **"Seeing through my Father's eyes."** It summarizes the goal and purpose for each person reading this book. Here are the words; see if you agree.

    I'm loving what I can see

    With His spirit alive in me

    I'm finding beauty for the first time

    Looking through my Father's eyes

    I can see your freedom coming

    (I can see your freedom coming)

    You'll be a slave to nothing

    (You'll be a slave to nothing)

    I'm finding beauty for the first time

    Looking through my Father's eyes

    (I'm finding beauty for the first time)

(Looking through my Father's eyes)

So many days I listen

To the voice inside my head

I never thought that I'd be

Someone who could be misled

I wanted the mirror to show me

Something I could not see

I needed explanations for expectations

I could never reach

I know I'm not the only one

Who's ever cried for help

And Jesus did for me

What I could not do myself

He changed my life

I'm changing my mind

He healed all that was broken inside

I'm loving what I can see

With His spirit alive in me

I'm finding beauty for the first time

Looking through my Father's eyes

(Looking through my Father's eyes)

From what I see, it looks like

You don't like yourself too much

When I hear you talk, it sounds like

You just feel like giving up

I know it's hard to see through

What this world will tell you

'Cause misconceptions

And false reflections will never be the truth

Just know I'm not the only one

Who's ever cried for help

Jesus loves you in ways

That you cannot love yourself

He changed my life

I'm changing my mind

He healed all that was broken inside

I can see your freedom coming

You'll be a slave to nothing

I'm finding beauty for the first time

Looking through my Father's eyes

2. **Voice of Truth** by Casting Crowns

"Oh, what I would do to have
The kind of faith it takes to climb out of this boat I'm in
Onto the crashing waves
To step out of my comfort zone
To the realm of the unknown, where Jesus is
And He's holding out His hand
But the waves are calling out my name
and they laugh at me
Reminding me of all the times I've tried before and failed
The waves they keep on telling me time and time again
"Boy, you'll never win, you'll never win"
But the voice of truth tells me a different story
The voice of truth says, "Do not be afraid!"
And the voice of truth says, "This is for my glory."
Out of all the voices calling out to me
I will choose to listen and believe the voice of truth
Oh, what I would do to have
The kind of strength it takes to stand before a giant
With just a sling and a stone
Surrounded by the sound of a thousand warriors

Shaking in their armor
Wishing they'd have had the strength to stand
But the giant's calling out my name
and he laughs at me
Reminding me of all the times I've tried
before and failed
The giant keeps on telling me time and time again
"Boy, you'll never win, you'll never win"
But the stone was just the right size
To put the giant on the ground
And the waves, they don't seem so high
On top of them looking down
I will soar with the wings of eagles
When I stop and listen to the sound of Jesus
Singing over me
The voice of truth tells me a different story
The voice of truth says, "Do not be afraid!"
And the voice of truth says, "This is
for my glory."
Out of all the voices calling out to me
(voices calling out to me)
I will choose to listen and believe
(I will choose to listen and believe)
I will choose to listen and believe the
voice of truth
I will listen and believe
I will listen and believe the voice of truth

I will listen and believe

'Cause Jesus, You are the voice of truth

And I will listen to You, You are"

Written by: Steven Curtis Chapman, John Mark Hall
Album: Casting Crowns
Released: 2003
Lyrics provided by Musixmatch

3. **"What the Hard times taught me"** by Jason Gray

Sometimes it feels like I learned to see in the dark

Like something came together when I fell apart

Getting up again when my knees were skinned

Showed me every end is where you hit restart

I wish there was an easy way

But I found the light in darker days

Yeah

I believe that I'm where you want me

I can see from the place you brought me

There's so much life in what the hard times taught me

Though it didn't go the way I planned it

I learned how to live open-handed

I came alive in what the hard times taught me

What the hard times taught me

Got me where you want me

What the hard times taught me

Got me where you want me

What the hard times taught me

Got me where you want me

Got me where you want me

Where you want me

Only the broken can tell you what healing is

When we're in need of forgiveness,
we learn to forgive

There's no rewind, just crooked lines

But Love is kind, and makes us whole again

I wish there was an easy way

But I found the light in darker days

Yeah

I'm wiser, and I'm kinder

Than I was before

It broke me, but you woke me

And I thank You Lord

I thank You Lord

What the hard times taught me

Got me where you want me

What the hard times taught me

Got me where you want me

Though it didn't go the way I planned

(What the hard times taught me)

I learned how to live open-handed

(Where you want me)

I came alive in what the hard times taught me

(Where you want me,
got me where you want me)

Writer(s): Jeff Sojka, Paul T. Duncan, Jason Gray

4. **"In Christ Alone"** written by Keith Getty and Stuart Townend, both songwriters of Christian Music in the United Kingdom

'In Christ alone my hope is found,
He is my light, my strength, my song;
this Cornerstone, this solid Ground,
firm through the fiercest drought and storm.
What heights of love, what depths of peace,
when fears are stilled, when strivings cease!
My Comforter, my All in All,
here in the love of Christ I stand.
In Christ alone! who took on flesh
Fullness of God in helpless babe!
This gift of love and righteousness
Scorned by the ones he came to save:
Till on that cross as Jesus died,
The wrath of God was satisfied –
For every sin on Him was laid;
Here in the death of Christ I live.
There on the ground, His body lay
Light of the world by darkness slain:
Then bursting forth in glorious Day
Up from the grave, he rose again!
And as He stands in victory
Sin's curse has lost its grip on me,
For I am His, and He is mine –

Bought with the precious blood of Christ.
No guilt in life, no fear in death,
This is the power of Christ in me;
From life's first cry to final breath.
Jesus commands my destiny.
No power of hell, no scheme of man,
Can ever pluck me from His hand;
Till He returns or calls me home,
Here in the power of Christ, I'll stand."

5. **Write Your Story** by Francesca Battistelli

They say
You're the King of everything
The One who taught the wind to sing
The source of the rhythm my heart keeps beating
And they say
You can give the blind their sight
And You can bring the dead to life
You can be the hope my soul's been seeking
I wanna tell you now that I believe it
I wanna tell you now that I believe it
I do, that You can make me new, oh
I'm an empty page
I'm an open book
Write Your story on my heart

Come on and make Your mark
Author of my hope
Maker of the stars
Let me be Your work of art
Won't You write Your story on my heart
Write Your story, write Your story
Come on and write your story, write your story
Won't You write Your story on my heart
My life
I know it's never really been mine
So do with it whatever You like
I don't know what Your plan is
But I know it's good, yeah
I wanna tell You now that I believe in
I wanna tell You now that I believe in
In You, so do what You do, oh
I'm an empty page
I'm an open book
Write Your story on my heart
Come on and make Your mark
Author of my hope
Maker of the stars
Let me be Your work of art
Won't You write your story on my heart
Write Your story, write Your story

Come on and write Your story, write Your story

Won't You write Your story on my heart

I want my history to be Your legacy

Go ahead and show this world

What You've done in me

And when the music fades

I want my life to say, ay yeah

I let You write Your story, write Your story

Write Your story, write Your story

Come on and write Your story; write Your story

Won't You write Your story on my heart

Written by: Francesca Battistelli, David Arthur Garcia, and Benjamin Glover
Album: If We're Honest
Released: 2014
Lyrics provided by Musixmatch

Ryan Stephenson grew up in a trailer in Bonanza, Oregon, a town of 420. He was extremely poor. He learned to love music at an early age and got a guitar at 18. After school, he sang and played at coffee shops and began working full-time in Boise, Idaho, as a Paramedic. One night, he responded to a 911 call of a woman killed by lightning. As they drove to pick up her dead body and take her to the hospital, Ryan prayed for her. When Ryan arrived, he administered the standard injection and heart massages, and she was revived. She was so grateful that after rehab, she befriended him and asked for a way to help him. He told her, ***"I have written these songs, and I don't have the money to record them."*** She said she had received an unexpected check and would pay for the five demo songs to be recorded at a studio. There, he met Toby Mac and introduced him to his song, ***"Speak Life."*** Toby recorded it, and it became a massive hit among Christian music. Toby even included him in a YouTube video. Later, Ryan recorded an album, and the tenth song was titled "Eye of the Storm," about his rugged life. It was no. 1 among Christian music for 16 weeks. For 16 weeks, that song was #1 on the Christian music charts. It launched his Christian music career. During Covid, he played in what he called 'back yards concerts' for families and neighbors to stay busy when most theaters were closed. Ryan says, ***"I pursue the will and glory of God. I keep praying, and God keeps opening new doors."***

Has God turned bad into good in your life?

6. **Speak Life** TobyMac

Some days, life feels perfect
Other days, it just ain't workin'
The good, the bad, the right, the wrong
And everything in between
Yo, it's crazy, amazing
We can turn our heart through the words we say
Mountains crumble with every syllable
Hope can live or die
So speak life, speak life
To the deadest, darkest night
Speak life, speak life
When the sun won't shine and
you don't know why
Look into the eyes of the brokenhearted
Watch 'em come alive as soon as you speak hope
You speak love, you speak
You speak life, oh, oh, oh, oh, oh
Some days, the tongue gets twisted
Other days, my thoughts just fall apart
I do, I don't, I will, I won't
It's like I'm drowning in the deep
Well, it's crazy to imagine
Words from my lips as the arms of compassion
Mountains crumble with every syllable

Hope can live or die
So speak life, speak life
To the deadest, darkest night
Speak life, speak life
When the sun won't shine and
you don't know why
Look into the eyes of the brokenhearted
Watch 'em come alive as soon as you speak hope
You speak love, you speak
You speak life, oh, oh, oh, oh, oh
Lift your head a little higher
Spread the love like fire
Hope will fall like rain
When you speak life with the words you say
Raise your thoughts a little higher
Use your words to inspire
Joy will fall like rain
When you speak life with the things you say
Lift your head a little higher
Spread the love like fire
Hope will fall like rain
When you speak life with the words you say
So speak life, speak life
To the deadest, darkest night
Speak life, speak life

When the sun won't shine and

you don't know why

Look into the eyes of the brokenhearted

Watch 'em come alive as soon as you speak hope

You speak love, you speak

You speak life, oh, oh, oh, oh, oh

Some days, life feels perfect

Written by: Toby Mckeehan, James L. Moore, Ryan Dale Stevenson
Album: Eye On It
Released: 2012

7. **You Say** Lauren Daigle

I keep fighting voices in my mind

that say I'm not enough

Every single lie that tells me

I will never measure up

Am I more than just the sum of every

high and every low

Remind me once again just who I am

because I need to know

Ooh-oh

You say I am loved when I can't feel a thing

You say I am strong when I think I am weak

And you say I am held when I am falling short

And when I don't belong, oh You say I am Yours

And I believe (I) Oh, I believe (I)

What You say of me (I) I believe

The only thing that matters now is everything
You think of me
In You, I find my worth; in You, I find my identity
Ooh-oh
You say I am loved when I can't feel a thing
You say I am strong when I think I am weak
And you say I am held when I am falling short
When I don't belong, oh, You say I am Yours
And I believe (I) Oh, I believe (I)
What You say of me (I) Oh, I believe
Taking all I have, and now I'm laying it
at Your feet
You have every failure, God;
you have every victory Ooh-oh
You say I am loved when I can't feel a thing
You say I am strong when I think I am weak
You say I am held when I am falling short
When I don't belong, oh, You say I am Yours
And I believe (I) Oh, I believe (I)
What You say of me (I) I believe
Oh, I believe (I) Yes, I believe (I)
What You say of me (I) I believe

Written by: Bebo Norman, Jason Ingram, Mike Donehey, Lauren Daigle, Paul Brendon Mabury
Album: Look Up Child
Released: 2018

8. **Spirit Lead Me**

Influence Music sung by Michael Ketterer

This is my worship
This is my offering
In every moment
I withhold nothing
I'm learning to trust You
Even when I can't see it
And even in suffering
I have to believe it
If You say, "It's wrong," then I'll say, "No"
If You say, "Release," I'm letting go
If you're in it with me, I'll begin
And when You say to jump, I'm diving in
If You say, "Be still," then I will wait
If You say to trust, I will obey
I don't wanna follow my own ways
I'm done chasing feelings
Spirit lead me, hmm
Oh, Spirit lead me
It felt like a burden
But once I could grasp it
You took me further
Further than I was asking
And simply to see You
It's worth it all

My life is an altar
Let Your fire fall
If You say, "It's wrong," then I'll say, "No"
If You say, "Release," I'm letting go
If you're in it with me, I'll begin
And when You say to jump, I'm diving in
If You say, "Be still," then I will wait
If You say to trust, I will obey
Teach me how to follow in Your way
I'm done chasing feelings
Spirit lead me, oh, yeah
Holy Spirit
(Spirit lead me) yeah, as you sing it out
Oh, Spirit, lead me
When all hope is gone
When all hope is gone
And Your word is all I've got
I have to believe
You still bring water from the rock
To satisfy my thirst
To love me at my worst
And even when I don't remember
You remind me of my worth
I don't trust my ways
I'm trading in my thoughts
I lay down everything

'Cause You're all that I want
I've landed on my knees
This is the cup You have for me
And even when it doesn't make sense
I'm gonna let Your Spirit lead
(Spirit lead me)
I'm gonna let Your Spirit lead
(Spirit lead me)
Come on, sing it out, here we go
Spirit lead me
If You say, "It's wrong," then I'll say, "No"
If You say, "Release," I'm letting go
If you're in it with me, I'll begin
And when You say to jump, I'm diving in
If You say, "Be still," then I will wait
If You say to trust, I will obey
You're the only truth, the life, the way
I'm done chasing feelings
Spirit lead me, yeah, yeah, oh
(Spirit lead me) Spirit, oh
Spirit lead me
Spirit lead me
Even when it doesn't make sense, oh
I'm gonna trust in You
I'm gonna trust in You, oh yeah, yeah
Spirit lead me

Written by: Michael Barkulis, Melody Noel, Gabriel Wilson,
Graham Moore, Whitney Taylor Medina, Michael Ketterer
Album: Touching Heaven
Released: 2018
Lyrics provided by Musixmatch

9. **Redeemed** *Big Daddy Weave*

Seems like all I could see was the struggle
Haunted by ghosts that lived in my past
Bound up in shackles of all my failures
Wondering how long is this gonna last
Then You look at this prisoner and say to me
"Son, stop fighting a fight, it's already been won"
I am redeemed; you set me free
So I'll shake off these heavy chains
Wipe away every stain,
now I'm not who I used to be
I am redeemed, I'm redeemed
All my life, I have been called unworthy
Named by the voice of my shame and regret
But when I hear You whisper,
"Child, lift up your head"
I remember, "Oh God, You're not done with me yet"
I am redeemed, You set me free
So I'll shake off these heavy chains

Wipe away every stain,
now I'm not who I used to be
Because I don't have to be
the old man inside of me
'Cause his day is long dead and gone
Because I've got a new name, a new life,
I'm not the same
And a hope that will carry me home
I am redeemed, You set me free
So I'll shake off these heavy chains
Wipe away every stain,
'cause I'm not who I used to be
I am redeemed, You set me free
So I'll shake off these heavy chains
Wipe away every stain, yeah,
I'm not who I used to be
Oh, God, I'm not who I used to be
Jesus, I'm not who I used to be
'Cause I am redeemed
Thank God, redeemed

Written by: Michael Weaver, Benji Cowart
Album: Love Come To Life
Released: 2012

Robbie Trice learned to play the guitar at 13 and gave his life to Christ in high school. He and his buddies formed Kinfolk in 1971 and started playing in churches and coffee houses in Jacksonville, FL.

One day, he was sitting on the floor in his bedroom with his guitar and had a Holy Spirit moment. He had just started strumming and liked what he had heard, so he grabbed his King James Bible and looked for inspirational lyrics. He came upon Revelation 21, and the third verse said, ***"I heard a great voice out of heaven saying behold the Tabernacle of God is with men."*** He said, "Wow, this is working. I'm not having to change a lot of words around to fit the melody. It's even rhyming when he got to the first ***"he is the Alpha and Omega, the beginning and the end,"*** and that song naturally lifted into another level of energy. He began to think of Jesus's names, which all happened in 20 minutes.

He knew very little about crafting or writing a song. He believed the Lord God was giving him thoughts, words, and music. He was so honored that the Lord would give him that inspiration. Robbie and his wife, Martha, had attended a Bill Gaither concert and had the opportunity to introduce this song to their drummer. They were so touched and impressed that they bought his rights to the song.

To this day, the Gaither vocal band opens every concert with ***"Alpha and Omega"***, and it has had 20 million views on YouTube and re-recorded 13 different CDs and videos, some of which have gone gold and platinum. Oh, how can God lead us who are open to His voice and thoughts in our soul and spirit?

Notice below some of Robbie's original notes from the song and cords.

ALPHA AND OMEGA

```
G                                   D
I HEARD A GREAT VOICE OUT OF HEAVEN SAYING,
   C                          Dsus        D
"BEHOLD THE TABERNACLE OF GOD IS WITH MEN.
G                              D
HE SHALL DWELL WITHIN IN THEM, THEY SHALL BE
                  C                      Dsus D (Gsus, G)
HIS PEOPLE, AND ALMIGHTY GOD WILL BE WITH THEM.

     G                         D
2) "HE SHALL WIPE AWAY ALL TEARS FROM THEIR EYES,
C                            Dsus  D
THERE SHALL BE NO MORE DEATH.
               G                      D
NEITHER SORROW NOR CRYING, AND NO MORE PAIN;
       C                              Dsus D
THE FORMER THINGS ARE ALL PASSED AWAY."

    A                       E
3) HE THAT SAT UPON THE THRONE SAID, "BEHOLD.
D                         Esus E
I MAKE ALL THINGS NEW."
A                 E                        D
HE SAID UNTO ME, "WRITE THESE WORDS, FOR THEY ARE
                  Esus E
FAITHFUL AND TRUE."
            A A9sus/G ,  D(2) A      A A9sus/G    D(2) A
AND IT IS DONE, IT IS DONE, IT IS DONE, IT IS DONE!
D/E
(CHORUS)      A                             E
HE IS THE ALPHA AND OMEGA, THE BEGINNING AND THE END;
     D                                   E
THE SON OF GOD, THE KING OF KINGS, LORD OF LORDS,
HE'S EVERYTHING!
     A                         E
MESSIAH, JEHOVAH, THE PRINCE OF PEACE IS HE;
     D                                           Esus
THE SON OF MAN, SEED OF ABRAHAM, SECOND PERSON
        E    D/E
IN THE TRINITY!  (REPEAT CHORUS)
```

ROBBIE TRICE, GAITHER VOCAL BAND

Are you a Movie star or a Jesus Disciple?

Denzel Washington, Academy Award winner has had an "epic & powerful Christian testimony that shows when you truly Put God First, the Lord Jesus (Yeshua) Christ can do great things in your life.

The Bible declares in (Proverbs 3: 5-6), ***"Trust in the Lord with all your heart, and lean not on your own understanding; In all your ways acknowledge Him, and He shall direct your paths." The Bible also declares in (Romans 10: 9-10), "That if you confess with your mouth the Lord Jesus and believe in your heart that God has raised Him from the dead, you will be saved. For with the heart one believes unto righteousness, and with the mouth, confession is made unto salvation."***

In his own words, ***"I've felt the hand of God in my life, no doubt about it. I remember sitting in my mother's beauty parlor in Mount Vernon, N.Y., on March 27, 1975, and in the mirror, I kept seeing this woman looking at me."*** Denzel Washington was then 20, a student at Fordham University in the Bronx.

"I was doing so bad in school, and this woman said, 'Somebody give me a piece of stationery! I'm having a prophecy!' I still have that piece of paper. 'You're going to speak to millions of people,' she told me. 'You're going to do great things!' And I thought, Yeah, right.

When's that going to start? On Monday? I'm flunking out of school."

Today, he has a voice that can reach millions.

***Put God First. Make Jesus (Yeshua)
Christ your Lord & Savior and Watch
what He does with your life!"***

Epilogue

Summary of the key points of this book

I want to share with you what I consider to be the main conclusions to this book

1. God has given us Words as His greatest tool to create, change, and command things to be in His plan for us to influence, love, and praise. God's being is in His Words. The Words of the Bible are His Spirit. Ultimately, Words are His tool for goodness and righteousness among all men and women on earth. He spoke the world into existence ref. In Genesis 1:3, God said, "Let there be light to and then in Genesis 1:26, God said let us create Man in our image."
   Godly words are in His will to be about the good things of God. His words and thoughts can overcome evil. He asks us to praise Him, which honors Him and is what the enemy hates and repels. If we live with our selfish pride, we make ourselves vulnerable to evil.
2. Obviously, in this world, an evil spirit is working among all societies to take us down and destroy the works of God. Jesus came to break the power of Evil. Without surrendering to Christ and his leading, many of us will live in pain, suffering, doubt, fear, and anxiety. We will hear words

like "You will never make it," "You are stupid," "No one loves you" etc. We have a toxic world, perpetuated a lot by today's news media and big organizations, and moral ignorance and decline. Evil thinking, doubts, or fears that help groups accomplish their goals are often about making more money or prejudice.

3. I have searched the Bible for the top words listed most often, and yes, the word God comes up 3,978 times. Next is the word Jesus 1,310 times. Love 656 times. Heaven 626 times. Evil 430 times. Mercy 126 times. Grace 124. To me, this says the Lord is calling us to live in Faith and righteousness by His Spirit of the good news and avoid the torture and fearful thoughts of evil or prideful thinking.
   — ***Philippians 4:8***— *"Finally, brethren, whatever is true, whatever is honorable, whatever is right, whatever is pure, whatever is lovely, whatever is of good repute, if there is any excellence and if anything worthy of praise, dwell (think) on these things."*

4. We have a Body, Soul, and Spirit. The largest part of each of us is a spirit because God is a Spirit and He created each of us.
   —***Jeremiah 29:11-13***— *"For I know the plans that I have for you,' declares the LORD, plans for welfare and not for calamity to give you a future and a hope. Then you will*

call upon Me and come and pray to Me, and I will listen to you. You will seek Me and find Me when you search for Me with all your heart."

God can speak to everyone but so does the power of evil. Do you know His voice vs. fear or demeaning thoughts of the evil one? But the Bible says we must be Born of the Spirit by surrendering to Christ to hear and recognize his Spirit speaking to us.

5. Very few Pastors describe the difference between the soul, the spirit, and the body. Still, I'm convinced that between 40 and 50% of our decision-making is through Spiritual and Nutritional solutions. I estimate that only 25% of Christian believers are committed to Christ in a personal relationship, having asked for forgiveness of their sins and asking for His daily leading of their lives. The key is to ask for wisdom, knowledge, and discernment, not to run the doctors, use drugs, or participate in immoral acts or other toxic things or thinking. They are more often spiritual battles, fears, insecurities, or issues that deceive our soul and or feel in our physical body.
6. Jesus came to preach the good news of the Kingdom of Heaven. Our destination is to be in heaven one day but manifest "heaven done on earth as it is heaven," referencing Matthew 4:17 where "Light overcomes darkness." The Light is the Spirit

of God, and the love of God is found in the Word of God and the praise of God.

7. Praise is a transformative act that requires our heart, our spirit, and our soul to engage in a spirit of love for Jesus Christ. It shifts our focus from the daily struggles to the love of Christ, who is to be our dwelling place in our Spirit with His Spirit. As we sing and praise, we see through the eyes of goodness, kindness, wisdom, knowledge, and love of Father and Son.

8. Some people are caught up in their daily lives, living in darkness, physical pain, and suffering, and our medical system feeds through fees or government subsidies. I don't believe in mental health; I believe in Spiritual health. Again, we are the first spirit. Without a personal relationship with Christ, there is not a full sense of love. While mainline denominations are decreasing, the music industry that focuses on praising God is expanding rapidly. Some quote declines in church attendance, yet at concerts, churches, Apple tunes, YouTube, and other media outlets, Praise Music is booming. One song by Jesus Culture received almost 400,000,000 views in five years on YouTube, more than the United States population. I suggest that heartfelt praise music is equal to or better than church attendance. Personal Bible study or small groups can teach or impact us more than an

average church service.

—***Matthew 6:9*** *— "Jesus said, "Pray, then, in this way: 'Our Father who is in heaven, Hallowed be Your name. 10 'Your kingdom come. Your will be done, On earth as it is in heaven."*

What do they do in heaven? They praise God. Why did God create us? To love us and be loved. Speaking and praising Him is loving him just as the angels and choir do in heaven. When you have thoughts of evil or worry or doubt or fear, Praise His Name, which is the title of one of the songs I've included in this book. Good praise hymns are just as good. My wife and I sing the doxology every morning. The Bible says the Word of God is stronger than a double sword. It's our way of cutting through evil and penetrates our spirit and soul.

—***Matthew 10:34***— *"Do not think that I came to [a] bring peace on the earth; I did not come to bring peace, but a sword."*

9. So praise His name and Word out loud and in song and worship in prayer as the aroma of God. Then your troubles and "stinking thinking" will decrease and fall away, particularly as you commanded. Don't listen to the toxic words of fear from the enemy.

   — ***2 Corinthians 2:15*** —*"For we are to God the pleasing aroma of Christ among those who are* *being saved and those who are perishing."* Satan hates the aroma of God and flees to find others prey upon.

10. As I quoted earlier, Dr. Darlene Lobel, a Neurosurgeon and Scientist, says, "When listening to or participating in loving music, dopamine is released. It's a hormone that causes your body to start to feel good, especially in your brain cells, and it elevates your mood and instantly makes you feel happier."
    — ***John 4:23*** — *"God seeks those who will worship Him with sincerity and authenticity."*

11. This book is full of examples because I think that is where many Pastors fail to witness real stories. s teach the principals but don't always give you an example of realistic application in a personal life, family, or even work. Live your life loving God and have heaven be part of your earthly experience.
    — ***2 Corinthians 3:17*** *17— "Now the Lord is the Spirit, and where the Spirit of the Lord is, there is liberty."*
    — ***Isaiah 48:13*** *—"Surely My hand founded the earth, And My right hand spread out the heavens; When I call to them, they stand together."*
    — ***Isaiah 49:13*** — *"Shout for joy, O heavens! And rejoice, O earth! Break forth into joyful shouting, O mountains! For the LORD has comforted His people And will have compassion on His afflicted."*

—***Isaiah 51:16*** *— "I have put My words in your mouth and have covered you with the shadow of My hand, to establish the heavens, to found the earth, and to say to Zion, 'You are My people.'"*

— ***Isaiah 55:9*** *— "For as the heavens are higher than the earth, So are My ways higher than your ways And My thoughts than your thoughts."*

— ***Malachi 3:10*** *— "Bring the whole tithe into the storehouse, so that there may be food in My house, and test Me now in this," says the LORD of hosts, "if I will not open for you the windows of heaven and pour out for you a blessing until it overflows."*

— ***Matthew 3:16*** *— "After being baptized, Jesus came up immediately from the water; and behold, the heavens were opened, and he saw the Spirit of God descending as a dove and lighting on Him,"*

— ***Matthew 3:17*** *— "and behold, a voice out of the heavens said, "This is My beloved Son, in whom I am well-pleased."*

— ***Matthew 4:17*** *— From that time Jesus began to preach and say, "Repent, for the kingdomof heaven is at hand."*

Some Influencers and Resources We Learned From

- ✓ The Bible (NIV and New Am Standard)
- ✓ Personal experiences from Lord's leading/speaking to me
- ✓ Full Gospel Businessmen International
- ✓ Wise Counsel Boot Camp speakers (150)
- ✓ Testimonies/interviews/speakers and clients (300)
- ✓ YouTube stories and 700 Club online
- ✓ Inspiration 316 Radio Show content by John Beehner
- ✓ Guidepost Magazine
- ✓ God Calling A.J. Russell editor, Barbour Publishing
- ✓ Prayers that Avail Much, Germaine Copeland
- ✓ Cancer Centers of America
- ✓ Leadership Bible edited by Ken Boa
- ✓ The Lord's leading and breaking my pride
- ✓ Gateway Bible online
- ✓ You Version Bible App

- ✓ The Christian Healing Ministry, Francis and Judith McNutt
- ✓ Previous Books I have written, including
  - ✓ True Wealth by the Book
  - ✓ Freedom Revolution Rocking our World
  - ✓ The Untold Secret that creates True Wealth
  - ✓ The Rock Solid Leadership Blueprint, Resource Guide
- ✓ Bible Studies, 12 Pastors including Paul Zink. Ricky Roberts, Russ Austin, Doug Rutt, Charles Stanley, Joyce Meyer, Tony Evans
- ✓ WAYRadio, Jacksonville Florida Bible Teaching
- ✓ Steve Strang, Charisma Media
- ✓ Henry Blackaby, Experiencing God
- ✓ Howard Dayton, Crown Financials Ministry
- ✓ Ron Blue Kingdom Advisors
- ✓ Pat Morley, Man in the Mirror
- ✓ Bill Mc Combes, Counselor and Coach
- ✓ Al Hollingsworth, Aldelano Packaging
- ✓ Stu Epperson, Salem Radio Network

THANK YOU!

Leaders we quoted or whose stories we share

Bill Bowerman

Bill Bright

Mark Burnett

Jim Carrey

Truett Cathy

Jan Christie

Germaine Copeland

Henry Crowell

Loren Cunningham

Cecil B. DeMille

Phil Driscoll

Thomas Edison

Dick Erickson

Jim Francis

Millard Fuller

David Hairabedian

Jon Heyman

Conrad Hilton

Tom Hill

Guy Iannello

Steve Jobs's

Hugh Jones

Max Karrer

Pat Kelly

Marlene Klepees

Phil Knight

Ed Kobel

James Kraft

Dr. Caroline Leaf

Dr. Darlene Lobel

Jack Manilla

John Maisel

Rollo May

Francis McNutt

Judith McNutt

Pat Morley

Pam Mullarkey

Tony Nasrallah

Bob Nourse

James Cash Penney

Derek Prince

Bill Riddell

John D. Rockefeller Sr.

Ricky Roberts

Jordan Rubin

Kathi Smith

Steven Spielberg

Jack Stack

Ryan Stephenson

Bud Toole

Robbie Trice

Don Wass

Denzel Washington

Tom Watson

Daniel Williams

Bob Williamson

Oprah Winfrey

Steve Wozniak

Zig Ziglar

John Beehner

CEO and Founder of Wise Counsel

John Beehner is a seasoned entrepreneur, author, mentor, and radio personality who has dedicated nearly 40 years to empowering business leaders and ministry executives. He founded ***TEC*** (The Executive Committee) Florida in 1981, today known as Vistage, a platform that allowed him to engage with numerous CEOs of fast-growing small to mid-sized companies. John guided his clients through a round-table process of problem-solving, focusing on quality, service, and profitability. After 13 successful years, he sold the business and established ***Wise Counsel*** in 1999 to assist entrepreneurs and ministry executives of faith in balancing their business and spiritual calling.

John has authored four books on Christians in the marketplace, including ***"True Wealth by the Book"*** and ***"The Untold Secret that Creates True Wealth."*** These books highlight the experiences of pioneers and icons such as J.C. Penney, Sam Walton, Mary Kay, and Conrad Hilton. He has also created a video-based training series titled ***'How and Why Good Business Creates True Wealth,'*** which is filled with inspiring stories and examples of individuals who were motivated by their faith to build successful companies.

In 2021, John published ***"The Rock Solid Leadership Blueprint,"*** which focuses on building a business on Biblical principles. The book features over 50 experts and resources to help and inspire leaders to implement the 7 Cornerstones of a Solid Foundation. John is highly respected in the Christian business community and has hosted two radio shows, sharing his insights and experiences with his audience. John Beehner's dedication to guiding entrepreneurs and ministry leaders towards success, while integrating faith and business, has made him a respected figure in the industry. His wealth of knowledge and practical wisdom continue to inspire and empower those who seek to build thriving organizations grounded in biblical principles.

Made in the USA
Columbia, SC
01 October 2024

42698661R00124